Hype for Alex Coles's *Cro*

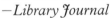

"This is an intriguing stud[
who were inspired by Sin[
look at an influential elem[
—*Library Journal*

"A satisfying historical survey of crooners [...]
Music history buffs will be riveted."
—*Publishers Weekly*

"The chapters on each of the ten artists collectively
give the reader a better appreciation of an often
satirized or misunderstood musical style.
In that way, *Crooner* contributes to the literature
on popular music."
—*PopMatters*

"*Crooner* [...] has the virtue of sending you back
to the songs and albums Coles discusses."
—*Mail on Sunday*

"Crooning [...] is an extremely broad church, as
Alex Coles's new book on the subject shows us."
—*The Quietus*

"Coles's post-critical writing delivers a rich, vibrant
genealogy of crooning, while also holding court
in academic circles."
—*Popular Music and Society*

Hype for Alex Coles's *Tainted Love:*
From Nina Simone to Kendrick Lamar:

"Author Alex Coles […] selects eleven songs that go
far beyond the archetypal 'moon in June' material […]
The concept is deftly considered […] while the song
choices are often inspired."
—*Irish Times*

"Alex Coles manages to uncover even more depth
and beauty in these songs than I thought possible."
—Jeremy Deller

"*Tainted Love* is like a new set of speakers, revealing
nuances of lyric and sound in familiar songs. Coles is
an uncommonly sensitive listener; his writing always
invites you back to the music itself."
—Adam Bradley, RAP Lab, UCLA

"Alex Coles began as an art critic, probed the
relationship between design and art, and emerges here
in a new guise as a music writer. Coles listens as hard,
and hears just as incisively, as he once used to look.
Tainted Love's essays are highly personal, meticulously
researched love songs to a musical subgenre suffused
with complex and often awkward emotions."
—Rick Poynor

"This is the perfect music book."
—Chris Hawkins, BBC Radio 6 Music

Fusion!

Fusion!

From Alice Coltrane to Moor Mother

Alex Coles

Sternberg Press

For Nesty

As Alice Coltrane taps out a fuzzy sound on the Wurlitzer and Carlos Santana strikes a soaring note on the guitar, jazz and rock momentarily fuse. From the 1960s to today, fusions like theirs are essential to the very vitality of contemporary and popular music. Acting as a catalyst more than any other genre, jazz mixes with genres of contemporary and popular music from bossa nova and rock to pop and hip-hop. When these genres expand and contract with the passage of time, the nature of the fusion changes. The exchange between them triggers the dynamic tension essential to fusion, whether it's saxophonist Kamasi Washington pushing rapper Kendrick Lamar or rock singer Lou Reed stretching trumpeter Don Cherry. Without fusion, their music, individually and collectively, wouldn't be as rich as it is.

Musicians pursue fusion as a process to confront and embrace changing generations, eras, philosophies, sensibilities, idioms, histories, and geographies. Where Miles Davis fuses jazz and rock to engage with the counterculture of a younger generation in the late 1960s, Moor Mother harnesses fusion to access the way key figures in jazz history form a community. Where it allows Lamar the opportunity to deal with acute feelings of guilt, it lends Joni Mitchell pivotal agency as she matures;

and where it guides Lora Logic into crafting a unique voice amid the male-dominated post-punk genre, it gives Herbie Hancock the tools to explore East Asian culture.

Driven by process, collaboration is key to the examples chosen for *Fusion! From Alice Coltrane to Moor Mother*, with each chapter foregrounding the coming together of two or more figures. To reflect this, besides those attributed to bands (which are collaborative by nature), the tracks-cum-chapters are headed under at least two names, even if the song was released under just one.

Fusion! seeks to push beyond the ubiquitous label "jazz fusion." Treating fusion as a static style rather than an ongoing process, academics and journalists have attempted to ascribe specific attributes to it, fixing amorphous and fluid work within a single term.[1] All labels can be limiting, but jazz fusion is particularly so. That the video game *Grand Theft Auto IV* (2008) features a radio station named "Fusion FM" playing smooth, funk-inflected jazz gives a sense of how static jazz fusion is in the popular imagination. By no surprise, each of the musicians included here are acutely aware of the pitfalls of treating fusion as style. Davis derisively refers to "what the critics later would call fusion"; Hancock recalls being frustrated once his music "wound up with a jazz fusion label on it"; and Mitchell is disparaging when "producers push jazz in a fusion direction."[2]

Although many of the names often associated with fusion can be found in these pages, they're not necessarily in their anticipated places. Several of the tracks sit in the margins of the musician's oeuvre: instead of with the million-selling 1973 *Head Hunters* LP, Hancock appears in a collaboration with the pop singer Kimiko Kasai, and rather than the critically praised 1975 LP *Brown Rice*, Cherry turns up in his overlooked collaboration with Reed. Also, the fusions this book brings into focus center on the human voice as an instrument. This tips the contents toward popular music, where voice consistently plays a central role. Tracks featuring both a vocalist and horn player tend to emphasize this symbiosis, with Lamar inventively playing off Washington, and Mitchell off Shorter.

The chronology starts in 1969 with Davis piloting the dialogue between acoustic jazz and the electric folk rock of the Byrds with the track "In a Silent Way." Working with young musicians willing to embrace the electric instruments associated with rock, Davis's fusion of genres is realized by way of his unique ability to work intergenerationally. Other musicians had already fused jazz with rock, but Davis's remains the most significant as it emphasizes process over style.[3] In the same year as "In a Silent Way," the overlooked collaboration between Eumir Deodato and Antonio Carlos Jobim with Frank Sinatra on "Wave" leads to a fusion of the Americas, while three years later, when Coltrane and Santana collaborate on the track "Angel of Sunlight," the fusion of jazz and rock emerges from their fusion of spiritual paths.

In 1979, Hancock and Kasai fuse funk-laced jazz with pop on "Butterfly," using their collaboration as a vehicle to question the dominance of stereotypes of Eastern and Western cultures by inverting them, with Kasai incorporating a vocal style associated with a 1950s North American jazz singer and Hancock being informed by her brand of Japanese pop, reflected on his subsequent LPs. Also in 1979, Cherry and Reed's fusion of free jazz and new wave on "The Bells" flows from their fusion of philosophies, pushing beyond the New Age spiritualism and nihilism previously occupying them. Three years later, Logic's fusion of sensibilities leads to a fusion of free jazz and post-punk.

These musicians all fuse jazz with a relatively young genre. When "In a Silent Way," "Wave," and "Angel of Sunlight" were recorded, rock was still coalescing as a genre and very receptive to a dialogue with jazz, in turn rendering jazz open to a dialogue with rock (especially as jazz was then at its lowest commercial ebb and rock at its highest). Similarly, in 1979, Japanese city pop and post-punk were brand new when "Butterfly" and "The Bells" were recorded.

In the early 1990s compelling fusions of jazz with hip-hop emerged, typified by A Tribe Called Quest's "Can I Kick It?," a track that uses a jazz-inflected sample to drive the band's fusion of genres. Jazz and hip-hop are further fused two-and-a-half decades later by Lamar, with "u," on which he and Washington bring together contrasting musical histories of South Central Los Angeles. Meanwhile, Neneh Cherry's 2018 "Natural Skin Deep," realized with Four Tet, fuses her personal trajectory through the genres of post-punk, hip-hop, and electronica. By merging the tenor saxophone associated with Pharoah Sanders and the trance-like beats of Detroit techno, the Comet Is Coming's 2022 "Pyramids" fuses spiritual jazz with electronic music. With backgrounds in very different genres, the collaboration between the three musicians makes for an engrossing example of fusion. Released the same year, Moor Mother's "Jazz Codes" fuses free jazz and hip-hop by bringing together historic jazz communities with her contemporary community in Philadelphia. Unlike jazz's fusion with rock when the genre was young, jazz's fusion with hip-hop—initially by A Tribe Called Quest and later by Lamar, Cherry, and Moor Mother—finds hip-hop most receptive once it has matured. Similarly, the Comet Is Coming arrive at EDM only when the genre has evolved.

As an artist-centered book, the songs selected are driven by a dynamic sonic or compositional principle coined by the musicians themselves. Where Davis "ventilates" compositions, Mitchell runs instruments "out of phase"; while A Tribe Called Quest inject "space" into a track, Lamar perpetually brings together "extremes"; and where Reed pursues the "dissonant," Moor Mother breathes a "dusty" quality into the grooves of her tracks.[4]

The depth and breadth of its trajectory from the late 1960s to the present demonstrates the dynamism of fusion when understood as a process. And while the mainstream music business's current fascination with jazz (peaking with the Ezra Collective being the first jazz group to win the prestigious Mercury Prize in 2023) is bound to fade, fusion will continue to be a vital means of creative expression.

1. For an academic account of fusion-as-genre, see Fabian Holt, "Jazz and Jazz-Rock Fusion," in *Genre in Popular Music* (Chicago, IL: Chicago University Press, 2007), 81–101. For a recent journalistic approach, see the *Wax Poetics* editorial "Jazz Confusion: The History of Jazz Fusion?" (December 17, 2021), https://www.waxpoetics.com/article/the-history-of-jazz-fusion/.

2. Miles Davis with Quincy Troupe, *Miles: The Autobiography* (London: Picador, 1990), 279; Herbie Hancock with Lisa Dickey, *Herbie Hancock: Possibilities* (London: Penguin Books, 2014), 221; Michelle Mercer, *Footprints: The Life and Work of Wayne Shorter* (London: Penguin Books, 2007), 219.

3. See Kai Winding's *Penny Lane & Time* (Verve, 1967) and Wes Montgomery's *A Day in the Life* (A&M, 1967).

4. Herbie Hancock commenting on Davis, quoted in John Szwed, *So What: The Life of Miles Davis* (London: Arrow Books, 2002), 240; Joni Mitchell, quoted in Vic Garbarini, "60 Minutes with Joni Mitchell," in *Joni on Joni: Interviews and Encounters with Joni Mitchell*, ed. Susan Whitall (Chicago, IL: Chicago Review Press, 2019), 199; Q-Tip, Red Bull Music Academy (conversation, 2013), https://www .redbullmusicacademy.com/lectures/q-tip; Kendrick Lamar, quoted in Colin Stutz, "Kendrick Lamar's Latest Album Wasn't Always Called *To Pimp a Butterfly*," *Billboard* (March 31, 2015); Lou Reed, quoted in David Fricke, "Lou Reed: The Rolling Stone Interview," *Rolling Stone* (May 4, 1989), https://www.rollingstone.com/music/music-news/lou -reed-the-rolling-stone-interview-2-174015/; Camae Ayewa, quoted in Madison Bloom, "Moor Mother on How Her New Album is a Gateway to Radical Thought," *Pitchfork* (September 2, 2021), https://pitchfork .com/thepitch/moor-mother-black-encyclopedia-of-the-air-interview/.

Miles Davis and John McLaughlin, "In a Silent
Way" (1969)

Generations

Miles Davis fuses genres by fusing generations,
collaborating with young jazz musicians who play
the electrified instruments associated with rock.[1]
Key to Davis's approach to fusion is the process of
"ventilating," as Herbie Hancock, one of the keyboard
players on the track, characterizes it, a technique the
trumpeter uses to introduce space into a composition

and its execution.[2] The collaboration on "In a Silent Way" lends Davis a vital contemporaneity two decades after his debut solo recordings.

The hum of the electric amplifiers driving John McLaughlin's guitar and the trio of electric keyboards on the track—played by Hancock, Chick Corea, and Joe Zawinul—is the first thing you hear after the needle drop. The hum provides a warm electronic bed for both the acoustic instruments (Dave Holland's double bass, Wayne Shorter's soprano saxophone, and Davis's trumpet), the electric guitar, and the keyboards to lie on. Traditional approaches to playing jazz keyboard—chording, soloing, and vamping—are rejected as each musician applies just the lightest of touches. At just over the two-minute mark, Shorter's soprano saxophone announces the main theme, joined by the lyrical caress of Davis's trumpet for the final minute, taking the track to just over four minutes in total. The sense of space—not only between the different instruments but also the notes each one plays—is palpable. "In a Silent Way" develops a form of ambient music that emphasizes sonic texture set in deep space, leading to a heightening of the senses. To listen to the track and not feel is impossible.

The public nature of Davis's gradual embrace of the electric instruments associated with rock performs the fusion of genres and generations in real time. Davis seldom rehearsed this diverse and youthful band for gigs or recordings, preferring the musicians to experiment, and even make mistakes, both onstage and in the recording studio. Each of the musicians Davis invited to play on "In a Silent Way" were in their twenties at the time of the track's recording. Where Davis cut his teeth on bebop in the 1940s, they all came of age two decades later in the mid-1960s, at the dawn of rock. In a period when the urban code was "don't trust anyone over thirty" — the drummer Tony Williams was the same age as Davis's eldest son, then serving in Vietnam — the generation gap separating Davis from these musicians could have presented a problem. By harnessing the difference, Davis turns it into an asset.

Besides being a fusion of generations, Davis's band is a fusion of races, with Davis, Hancock, Shorter, and Williams all being African American, while Holland, McLaughlin, and Zawinul are white.[3] As an extension of the generational shift, Davis also embraces contemporary fashion, moving away from the preppy Brooks Brothers suits he once sported toward wearing African dashikis and robes in tune with the counterculture of the late 1960s.[4] Unlike the psychedelic cover of 1970's *Bitches Brew*, *In a Silent Way* features a conservative headshot of Davis taken by Lee Friedlander, a photographer of the contemporary social landscape. The moodiness of the image may reflect the ambient tone of the LP's title track, but the impact of the fusion of generations can only just be glimpsed, with Davis showing the beginnings of an afro, which becomes more pronounced with the turn into the 1970s.

To fully understand the origins of Davis's fusion of genres and generations, it's necessary to rewind to a moment when he describes his music as being in flux due to the impact of rock on it. "I was starting to think about other ways I could approach the music I wanted to play, because I could feel myself starting to want to change," writes Davis, knowing "it had something to do with the guitar."[5] Davis first features the electric guitar on "Circle in the Round," cut in December 1967 (and not released until much later on a collection of archive recordings). Dissatisfied with the guitarist Joe Beck, who plays on the track, Davis turned to George Benson early the following year and recorded "Paraphernalia," but Benson rejected the offer to join the band, and the guitar seat was not properly occupied until McLaughlin joins in early 1969. The youthful guitarist McLaughlin, and his emblematic rock instrument, drive Davis's fusion of genres.[6]

Davis describes also wanting the feel of the electric bass guitar, perhaps the instrument second most associated with rock, to feature in his work.[7] Played by either Ron Carter or Holland in 1968, the acoustic bass assumes the role of the electric bass when Corea or Hancock accompany it on their electric Fender Rhodes keyboards. With both the acoustic bass and the Fender Rhodes playing the bass line, as per the track "Filles de Kilimanjaro," Davis achieves a sound with the more defined bottom end associated with rock.

Though not yet embracing rock in recordings — his complete incorporation of the electric guitar was still to come — Davis certainly was listening to it earlier. Leonard Feather, editor of the jazz magazine *DownBeat*, writes of visiting Davis's hotel suite in 1968 and finding records and tape cartridges of the Byrds' music (among others).[8] The Byrds' guitarist David Crosby later reveals Davis's role in getting the band signed to his label, Columbia Records, a few years earlier in 1965. Listening to their demo, the Columbia executives went to Davis, who was on Columbia, and said, "'Miles, what do we do with these guys?' He said, 'sign them.'"[9] Ballads by the Byrds such as "Renaissance Fair" (1967) (featuring Crosby and Roger McGuinn on guitar, Chris Hillman on bass, and producer Paul Usher on keyboard), on their fourth LP for Columbia Records, *Younger Than Yesterday*, are especially pertinent to "In a Silent Way," as they, too, use a mixture of acoustic and electric instrumentation to create atmospheric textures.

A year after "In a Silent Way" was recorded, Davis lays down Crosby's composition "Guinnevere," composed after leaving the Byrds (released on Crosby, Stills & Nash's eponymous debut LP in 1969). "I'm standing in front of [jazz club] the Village Gate, and [Miles] walks up to me," recounts Crosby, and "[he] says, 'You Crosby?' I said 'yes,' 'I cut one of your tunes. [...] You want to hear it?'"[10] "I listened to it," Crosby recalls, and he told Davis that "it doesn't sound like 'Guinnevere.'"[11] Crosby advised Davis to change the name and get the publishing rights, which, apparently, "pissed him off."[12] So extreme is Davis's editing of "Guinnevere" that it brings the dialogue with the song's composer to an abrupt halt. Some attempts at fusion are misunderstood, even by youthful composers.

Besides drawing on contemporary music by the Byrds, Davis also takes a detour via his own orchestral LPs—including *Porgy and Bess* (1959) and *Sketches of Spain* (1960)—cut almost a decade earlier with arranger Gil Evans, producing a type of music that fused jazz and classical music referred to as "Third Stream."[13] What connects these LPs to "In a Silent Way" is how genres are combined to create atmospheric textures. "These records he made with Gil [Evans]," asserts McLaughlin, "[are] masterpieces of fusion."[14] To achieve this fusion, Davis takes the modal—a form of playing that emphasizes improvisational scales instead of traditional chords—developed with Evans to such an extreme that it opens onto the ambient, a type of music where even scales are eschewed in favor of pure texture. Recorded with Evans in early 1968, the rare (and at the time unreleased) track "Falling Water" gives a more accurate picture of Davis's gradual move toward fusing jazz with rock. Where other tracks from the period feature Evans's input, "Falling Water" is the only full collaboration documented between the two from the time. "Falling Water" features the duo experimenting with the electric instruments Davis was using elsewhere. In 1968, Evans's large orchestra provides the impetus for the sound of the mesh of electric and acoustic instruments on "In a Silent Way." The Fender Rhodes keyboard is critical to this. "I'm crazy about the way Gil Evans voices his music, so I wanted to get me a Gil Evans sound but in a small band," explains Davis, "[and] that required an instrument like the [Fender Rhodes], which can get all those different instrumental sounds."[15] Where the Byrds use a twelve-string Rickenbacker to give the impression of several guitars playing in unison to achieve a shimmering tone, Davis uses the Fender Rhodes to "sound like a full orchestra."[16] The degree of Davis's fusion of jazz with rock gradually becomes more pronounced with his experimentation with electric instruments. And it's at this point, in early 1969, that Davis decides to record "In a Silent Way." The track marks the moment when Davis's fusion of jazz and rock goes public.

To arrive at a version of "In a Silent Way" Davis deemed suitable for recording, Zawinul's composition required substantial editing. "The section of the tune he used, and which now has become famous," bemoans Zawinul later, "never had any changes, apart from a couple of chords going up. [...] I believe that Miles was wrong in taking these two chords out, because the tune does not have the climax it could have had."[17] But Davis's stripping back of "In a Silent Way" is central to making the composition an appropriate framework for fusion. Once dense, now the tune is full of space, courtesy of Davis listening to minimalist composers such as Terry Riley (*In C* was released in 1968) as well as the Byrds. Hancock describes how "[Miles] had the talent to draw out the best solos by ventilating the compositions [of others]."[18] Hancock's term "ventilating" captures how Davis pares away the superfluous in a composition to arrive at its bare structure.

Davis applies the process of ventilating not only to a composition but also to each musician's approach to playing it. In this sense, "In a Silent Way" marks a crucial point of transition: "I was getting away from using a lot of solos in my group sound," writes Davis, "[and] moving more toward an ensemble thing, like the [...] rock bands."[19] From "In a Silent Way" onward, Davis encourages the musicians in his band to eschew the usual theme/solo structure and instead work together as an ensemble. Ventilating musicians' playing could be difficult, but it was essential to fusion. Davis's approach to ventilating Hancock's keyboard work was communicated with the vague suggestion "don't play the butter notes."[20] "I was thinking," remembered Hancock, "butter is rich, what are the rich notes? [They're] the sounds that determine the character of a chord [...] so I struggled and tried to leave them out. The solo I played was jagged and too sparse, but I got it in two weeks."[21] Hancock's playing on "In a Silent Way" is as economic as it is subtle. The recording session for "In a Silent Way" was McLaughlin's first with Davis. "Miles didn't like [what I initially played] so he came up to me [...] and he said: 'Why don't you play it like you don't know how to play the guitar?' I thought, 'this is a good one: I should play it like I don't know how to play guitar?'"[22] The unusual suggestion worked, leading McLaughlin to ventilate his playing. The drone-like sound the guitarist achieves on "In a Silent Way" is beautiful in its simplicity.

The rehearsal of "In a Silent Way," made available on 2001's *The Complete In a Silent Way Sessions*, provides the listener with a portal into Davis's pursuit of fusion as process. For five-and-a-half minutes, Hancock, McLaughlin, Zawinul, and the rest of the ensemble go back and forth trying to locate the precise point where acoustic jazz fuses with electric rock. The role of the trumpet changes radically from the rehearsal to the final version, demonstrating how Davis ventilates his own playing. Where in the rehearsal the trumpet—along with Shorter's soprano saxophone—constantly repeats the main theme, in the released version Davis only appears in the last minute or so of the song. Entering at the very end with a vapor trail of notes allows Davis to subtly provide the track with the climax Zawinul felt was missing due to its simplification.

Where Davis realizes fusion by ventilating a composition and a musician's playing of it, producer Teo Macero—the same generation as Davis—does so by ventilating the actual recordings. Recalling the musique concrète of Edgard Varèse (who Macero studied under at Juilliard), this involved the physical splicing together of different sections to form the final track. "I was able to cut out the stuff that wasn't good, and piece something together from the rest," says Macero.[23] Macero cut the tape down to eight-and-a-half minutes on one side and nine-and-a-half on the other. Eighteen minutes was not, however, enough music for an LP, so Macero looped some segments to make it longer. The most noticeable edit Macero made is the repetition of four minutes and ten seconds of the ballad "In a Silent Way" after the mid-paced "It's About That Time." Together, the three segments span the entirety of side two of the LP. In another moment of fusion with rock, Macero's repeating of "In a Silent Way" points to how the jazz producer used the studio as a creative tool, as Gary Usher and the Byrds did in rock from the mid-1960s onward. Macero's doubling of "In a Silent Way" in its entirety is tantamount to if Usher repeated "Goin' Back" at the end of side two of *The Notorious Byrd Brothers* from the previous year— a feat too audacious even for rock at the time. Besides this, the crucial difference between the way rock and jazz producers used the studio is that Usher makes extensive use of overdubs—dropping guitar solos in and adding any number of sweeteners—whereas Macero identifies key passages of playing and edits the track around them.

Following its release, one can hear its immediate impact on its featured musicians, all of whom continued to incorporate elements of rock into jazz, typified in 1971 by both Hancock's *Mwandishi* and Shorter and Zawinul's "Milky Way" from *Weather Report*. More broadly, "In a Silent Way" plays a vital role in shaping the vast canvas of avant-garde-leaning rock of the 1970s, from Can's "Bel Air" (1973) through Tangerine Dream's *Phaedra* the following year, on to Brian Eno's ambient music later in the decade. Constantly propelling himself forward by emphasizing process, by the time these younger musicians were reacting to "In a Silent Way," Davis had already moved on. The type of rock impacting his next two LPs transitioned from the romantic, atmospheric texture of the Byrds to the snarly attack of Jimi Hendrix. By the time a term was coined for this kind of music—what Davis derisively refers to as "what the critics would later call 'fusion'"—he was elsewhere.[24] Davis's fusion of genres, achieved by collaborating with different generations, may have been triggered by rock, but the stimulus was returned with interest as he then influenced subsequent stages of rock music.

1. For more on Davis and fusion, see Gary Tomlinson, "Miles Davis, Musical Dialogician," *Black Music Research Journal* 11, no. 2 (Fall 1991): 249–64; and Greg Tate, "The Electric Miles (Part I)," *DownBeat* 50, no. 7 (July): 16–18, 62, and "The Electric Miles (Part II)," *DownBeat* 50, no. 8 (August): 22–24, 54.

2. Herbie Hancock, quoted in John Szwed, *So What: The Life of Miles Davis* (London: Arrow Books, 2002), 240.

3. See Jeremy A. Smith, "Sell It Black: Race and Marketing in Miles Davis's Early Fusion Jazz," *Jazz Perspectives* 4, no. 1 (2010): 7–33.

4. Davis accorded this shift to his relationship with the young funk singer Betty Mabry, who he would marry in 1968. See Miles Davis with Quincy Troupe, *Miles: The Autobiography* (London: Picador, 1990), 300.

5. Ibid., 278.

6. For an in-depth account of McLaughlin's role in fusion, see Kevin Fellezs, "Meeting of the Spirits: John McLaughlin," in *Birds of Fire: Jazz, Rock, Funk, and the Creation of Fusion* (Durham, NC: Duke University Press, 2011), 123–47.

7. Davis with Troupe, *Miles*, 279.

8. Leonard Feather, "The Practitioner as Preacher," in Leonard Feather and Ira Gitler, *The Encyclopedia of Jazz in the Seventies* (New York: Horizon Press, 1976), 33.

9. David Crosby, "David Crosby on Miles Davis," interview by Tom Cridland, uploaded on September 30, 2020, https://www.youtube.com/watch?v=EhP-TAZw3PE.

10. Ibid.

11. Ibid.

12. Ibid.

13. See Gunther Schuller, "Third Stream," in *Musings: The Musical Worlds of Gunther Schuller* (New York: Da Capo Press, 1999), 114–18.

14. John McLaughlin, "John McLaughlin on Miles Davis and the Recording(s) that Changed His Life," interview by Larry Appelbaum, June 2, 2012, https://www.youtube.com/watch?v=pg8hNhao1oY.

15. Davis with Troupe, *Miles*, 285.
16. Miles Davis, quoted in Ian Carr, *Miles Davis: The Definitive Biography* (London: Harper Collins, 1998), 250.
17. Joe Zawinul, quoted in Paul Tingen, "The Making of *In a Silent Way* and *Bitches Brew*," *Mojo*, no. 94, 2001. For more on Zawinul, see Brian Glasser, *In A Silent Way: A Portrait of Joe Zawinul* (London: As Long As It's Hot, 2009).
18. Hancock, quoted in Szwed, *So What*, 240.
19. Davis with Troupe, *Miles*, 309.
20. Hancock, quoted in Szwed, *So What*, 240.
21. Ibid., 240.
22. John McLaughlin, "Miles and *In a Silent Way*," uploaded on February 3, 2017, https://www.youtube.com/watch?v=4sB5UkrkMu4.
23. Teo Macero, quoted in Tingen, "The Making of *In a Silent Way* and *Bitches Brew*."
24. Davis with Troupe, *Miles*, 279.

2

Frank Sinatra, Antonio Carlos Jobim,
and Eumir Deodato, "Wave" (1969)

The Americas

Realized by fusing contemporary jazz with both bossa
nova and swing, "Wave" is a collaboration between
arranger Eumir Deodato, composer and musician
Antonio Carlos Jobim, and vocalist Frank Sinatra.
The key to their version of "Wave" is the way the trio
transmute the song from its original form as a lilting
bossa-nova ballad into a propulsive vehicle for fusion.

Recorded in February 1969, "Wave" opens with Jobim's strident acoustic guitar riff, followed by the woodwind picking out a top note and a trombone's deep reply. As the rhythm section kicks in and carries the track forward, Sinatra enters with the first line of the lyric ("Now close your eyes"). The final phrase of the last line of the chorus ("Whenever two can dream a dream together") finds Sinatra sounding an exceptionally low note, the word "together" feeling as if it's beneath even the one played by the bass and trombone. Well into middle age, Sinatra's voice developed from the level of the violin in the 1940s to the viola in the 1950s, right down to the cello by the late 1960s.[1] Deodato's arrangement effectively combines the light and floating quality of Jobim's playing with the weight of Sinatra's cello-like baritone.

Underscoring the trio's fusion of genres and their origins across the Americas is the mix of generations: at twenty-six Deodato is young enough to be in touch with the rock musicians of the time, while at forty-two Jobim is something of a midway point between Deodato and Sinatra, the crooner then in his mid-fifties. This was crucial because by the late 1960s, Jobim and Sinatra's popularity was on the wane, supplanted by Tropicália and rock, respectively. As arguably the only contemporary genre of popular music Sinatra could truly relate to (attempts to cover Joni Mitchell and Simon & Garfunkel songs during the same period find him floundering), bossa nova was essential to Sinatra keeping up with popular music. Similarly, contemporary jazz was crucial to Jobim remaining in-step with current music.

Taking place at the height of the Cold War, the trio's fusion of the Americas is not without its tensions. "The new beat has even reached the New Frontier," says the voice-over on the 1962 CBS documentary devoted to bossa nova, before cutting to footage of Jackie Kennedy hosting a bossa-nova concert at the White House.[2] "The bossa nova was born in Brazil but its parentage is mixed [as] it's the result of the marriage between native samba and American jazz."[3] While this narrative simplifies a complex situation, bossa nova is indeed a fusion of traditional samba and West Coast jazz, typified by Stan Getz's LP *The Soft Swing* (1957).[4] Primarily developed in Rio de Janeiro, bossa nova was first popularized locally with the release of 1959's *Black Orpheus*, its soundtrack featuring Jobim's songs. With the film's international popularity, in 1961 the North American guitarist Charlie Byrd visited Brazil on a trip sponsored by the US State Department, and on returning worked with the producer Creed Taylor and Getz on 1962's *Jazz Samba*, the first US-produced LP to feature Jobim's compositions. Jobim's first solo LP followed in 1963, and in 1964 bossa nova entered the mainstream with the hit "The Girl from Ipanema," lifted from the LP *Getz/Gilberto*. Taylor continued producing bossa nova releases, before leaving Verve in 1967 to form his own label, CTI Records, as a subdivision of A&M Records, eventually becoming an independent label in 1970. Taylor may not have been directly involved with 1969's "Wave" (Sinatra used his standby producer Sonny Burke for the project), but the collaboration would never have taken place without the work Taylor did earlier in the decade.

Partly to get closer to this creative and commercial activity but also driven away by the social turmoil caused by the CIA-sponsored overthrow of the left-leaning President João Goulart, in the late 1960s Jobim and Deodato relocated to North America.

Where exile forces them to embrace fusion, Sinatra remains in Los Angeles seeking out collaborations with younger songwriters and arrangers that could sustain his popularity. "Wave" may be a fusion of the Americas, but it's on North American terms.[5] With photographs taken by the art director and photographer Ed Thrasher—including an unused one of Sinatra standing in front of a Greyhound bus—the LP cover affirms this logic by depicting Sinatra alone, despite the collaborative nature of the project.

Jobim's first attempt at "Wave" in 1967, an instrumental arranged by Claus Ogerman and produced by Taylor, sounds tepid in contrast to the 1969 version. Featuring many of the same musicians, the difference between the two versions highlights how Jobim's musical vocabulary broadens in these two years, as he moves away from the smoothness associated with Ogerman (on the debut Taylor-produced LP *The Composer of Desafinado, Plays* from 1963) toward the expansive fusion of rock-inflected jazz and bossa nova on the solo albums with Deodato (the Taylor-produced *Tide* and *Stone Flower* from 1970).

The type of jazz incorporated into "Wave" is quite different from the jazz Jobim drew on earlier in the decade. Instead of the tight, brief tracks populating Miles Davis's *Birth of the Cool* (the LP spearheading the West Coast sound of the 1950s later played through by Getz), there's a sense of Deodato and Jobim now being guided by Davis's latest releases, especially the title tune of 1968's *Filles de Kilimanjaro*, with its subtle fusion of jazz and rock. "Wave" is the sound of the most contemporary kind of jazz just—and only just—beginning to embrace its fusion with rock.

By 1969 Deodato's relationship to Jobim's compositions is already extensive. Deodato's debut LP in 1964 is devoted to Jobim's songs, and their dialogue gains pace with their collaboration on 1966's *Love, Strings and Jobim*. After a gap of three years, Deodato works intensively with the composer from early 1969 on the Sinatra LP through *Stone Flower* and *Tide* toward the end of 1970. Thereafter, Jobim continues to be crucial to the development of Deodato's own sound, as the arranger's first solo LP recorded in North America, *Prelude* (1973), is not only released on CTI Records and produced by Taylor but also relies on many of the same musicians featured on *Stone Flower*. Fusing elements of rock and funk, *Prelude* and Deodato's subsequent spate of LPs for CTI Records take their point of departure from where the final collaboration with Jobim leaves off.

Sinatra and Jobim first worked together two years before "Wave." Orchestrated by Jobim's initial go-to arranger in the US, Ogerman, *Francis Albert Sinatra & Antonio Carlos Jobim* (1967) smoothly fuses bossa nova with Sinatra's métier of swing, with seven of the songs composed by Jobim and three drawn from the Great American Songbook. Irving Berlin's "Change Partners" is based on a similar tempo to "Wave" but is much softer, with Sinatra singing in hushed tones. As beautiful as Sinatra and Jobim's reading of Berlin's song is, without Deodato injecting contemporary jazz into their fusion of bossa nova and swing there's no tension.

Leading up to the LPs with Jobim, collaborations with Count Basie's swing band render explicit Sinatra's leaning toward jazz (after being schooled in swing by Harry James and Tommy Dorsey in the late 1930s and early 1940s). Typified by the infectious "Fly Me to the

Moon," Sinatra's second LP with Basie from 1964 is arranged by a youthful Quincy Jones, resulting in harder-driving swing. "[We took] songs [...] identified with very specialized kinds of backgrounds ... but we had to transmute them," Jones explains in the LP's liner notes, "because [...] you have to discard all superfluities and get to the bones of a song before you start building it again."[6] Originally made popular by Peggy Lee, Jones and Sinatra chose to uncouple "Fly Me to the Moon" from its past as a ballad and transform it into a swinger. The way they transmute the song—in the case of "Wave," from Jobim's initial tepid interpretation with Ogerman—is crucial to what Deodato and Jobim achieve with Sinatra in 1969.

Deodato implicitly commented on the tension between US and Latin American sensibilities: "[Sinatra] was not comfortable [... as] the Jobim songs are not like typical American songs."[7] The rhythm and meter of bossa nova is quite different from swing. "Sinatra got away with it on the first record [with Jobim]," Deodato insists, "but there's a sense from the way he sings that he's still attracted to that groove."[8] With dissonant ballads and challenging upbeat numbers, the results of Deodato's insistence on Sinatra fully incorporating bossa nova are mixed, typified by how tentative "One Note Samba" sounds and how awkward the phrasing on "This Happy Madness" is. "Wave" is one of the few truly successful upbeat tracks on the record, a success premised on its ability to convincingly harness fusion.

Jobim's playing of Deodato's light but propulsive arrangement carries Sinatra's heavy baritone, accentuated in the final seconds of "Wave" as the phrase "together" is repeated. The first time, the bass and drums perform a slightly syncopated pattern;

34

the second time the word is repeated, the original rhythmic pattern is returned to. The very notion of being "together" is crucial to the fusion achieved through the trio's collaboration: it's as if the lyrical conceit of "Wave" — a lover inviting their beloved to cast their cares aside and be propelled forward by the wave of their relationship — is carried into the fusion of both genres and geographies. At song's end, the repeat of the phrase "together" drives this home.

1. Lyricist Sammy Cahn originally made this observation concerning the shift in Sinatra's tone from the 1940s to the 1950s. See Will Friedwald, *Sinatra! The Song Is You: A Singer's Art* (New York: Simon & Schuster, 1995), 237–38.

2. *The New Beat*, directed by Russ Bensley, aired December 28,1962, CBS News Eyewitness, https://www.jobim.org/jobim/handle/2010/4405.

3. Ibid.

4. See Bryan Daniel McCann, *Getz/Gilberto* (London: Bloomsbury, 2019).

5. On US Cold War policy driving culture, see Serge Guilbault, *How New York Stole the Idea of Modern Art* (Chicago, IL: University of Chicago Press, 1983).

6. Quincy Jones, liner notes, Frank Sinatra, *It Might as Well Be Swing* (Reprise Records, 1964).

7. Eumir Deodato, "An Interview with Eumir Deodato," interview by Chris Read, WhoSampled, www.mixcloud.com/whosampled /eumir-deodato-interviewed-for-whosampledcom/.

8. Ibid.

3

Alice Coltrane and Carlos Santana,
"Angel of Sunlight" (1974)

Paths

Alice Coltrane and Carlos Santana mix jazz
and rock by fusing their respective paths to the
"Universal Tone," the latter's term for music's spiritual
dimension.[1] The fourteen-minute track "Angel of
Sunlight," from their collaborative LP *Illuminations*
(1974), is a showcase for the counterpoint between
their distinctive sounds on the Wurlitzer and electric

guitar. Where fusion acts as a potential conduit for Coltrane to reach a rock audience, it enables Santana to realize a meditative state without recourse to the hallucinatory drugs he'd previously relied on and now wanted to leave behind.[2]

Coltrane and Santana's collaboration was instigated prior to arriving in the studio. "We met for the first time in the spring of '73, when Alice invited me to come stay with her in Los Angeles."[3] Their routine during the visit informs their LP the following year: each evening, Santana listened to Coltrane speak about music and spirituality, and at three thirty in the morning she would play the harp while he meditated. As they tuned into each other's ways of working, the conditions for fusion ripened.

With the tamboura droning and the congas beating, "Angel of Sunlight" opens with one of Santana's customary sustained notes. After a brief pause, the guitar returns with an increased intensity. Following solos from Jules Broussard on soprano saxophone and Tom Coster on Hammond organ, at seven-and-a-half minutes in, Coltrane takes her first solo, eagerly pressing the keys of the Wurlitzer. Where Santana's tone soars upward, Coltrane's burrows down. Moving in opposite directions, they produce a counterpoint of sonic tones. Capturing this, the trippy LP cover features a painting by Michael Wood depicting beams of light emanating from two angels.

The spiritual teachings of the Indian gurus Swami Satchidananda Saraswati and Sri Chinmoy lead Coltrane and Santana to adopt the names Turiya and Devadip, respectively. Addressing thousands of rock fans onstage at Woodstock in 1969 (where Santana played while tripping on LSD), Satchidananda speaks of the Universal Tone, describing the celestial sound of contemporary music as the one "that controls the whole universe."[4] Coltrane introduces Santana to Satchidananda in 1973, but the guitarist is drawn more to Chinmoy, who he meets through John McLaughlin. Chinmoy encourages Santana to establish a more intimate relationship with the electric guitar, leading Santana to the realization that "a note has an aura, which comes from harmonics and overtones, and that's where your guitar personality comes from."[5] Meditation is key to bringing these notes together to establish the player's guitar persona. "If I feel myself scattered, pulling away from my core, if I feel the Universal Tone separating into different notes," then "[I chant] 'I am that I am. I am the light'" and focus is reestablished.[6]

Parallel with these spiritual teachings is John Coltrane and his tenor saxophone. After meeting in 1963 and marrying in 1965, from early 1966 until his death in 1967 Alice Coltrane is a vital part of John Coltrane's band. Playing together felt "as if you were to just walk out of this door and see a new world, a new universe with so many opportunities in it," she remarked.[7] Recorded while grieving, Coltrane's first solo LPs for Impulse! remains close to the feel of her late husband's quartet circa the mid-1960s. But by 1971, with the release of *Journey in Satchidananda* and *Universal Consciousness*, her harp, piano, and Wurlitzer playing develop in an entirely new direction.[8] On her subsequent LPs with Impulse!—1972's *World Galaxy* and 1973's *Lord of Lords*—Coltrane pursues an even more independent direction by using an ensemble of strings, her radical development culminating with *Illuminations* in 1974.

"The first thing I heard was [John] Coltrane's volume and intensity," remembers Santana, "[which] fit the times," the 1960s being characterized by the "very loud, violent darkness that came from the war and riots and assassinations."[9] Beginning with his debut LP in 1969, Santana introduced elements of Coltrane's sound into his guitar playing, continuing with 1970's *Abraxas* and 1971's *Santana III*.[10] With its intensity "it sounded like [Coltrane's] horn was putting holes in the darkness—each time he blew, more light came through."[11] The turn toward Eastern spiritual leaders is the direct result of a desire to draw light through the era's darkness. The precise guitar tone Santana achieves recalls tracks such as "India" (1961) where John Coltrane embraced the sitar playing of Indian classical musician Ravi Shankar.[12] By way of Coltrane's saxophone, Santana indirectly feeds Shankar into his guitar playing. Transposing the sound of the sitar into the electric guitar between 1967 and 1971, by 1972 Santana fully embraces jazz instrumentation, leading to that year's *Caravanserai*. Santana then doubles down on the jazz influence, returning to John Coltrane with 1973's tribute LP *Love Devotion Surrender*, recorded with McLaughlin. Inspired by Alice Coltrane's trajectory, it takes meeting her in 1973 and their collaboration in 1974 for Santana to move beyond the spectre of the saxophonist.

Prior to her collaboration with Santana, Coltrane ventures into rock by appearing on Laura Nyro's *Christmas and the Beads of Sweat* (1970) and the Rascals' *Peaceful World* (1970), then joining both onstage in 1971 at New York's Carnegie Hall to celebrate Satchidananda's birthday (this performance being released by Impulse! only in 2024). Three years later her interest in rock increases, leading to the collaboration with Santana. "We did those sessions at Capitol Studios in Los Angeles" and "everything was done live."[13] Coltrane notes that Santana "was so happy, so buoyant, such a beautiful soul," injecting a "youthful dynamic into everything that we did."[14] While their exchange is two-way, the breadth of Coltrane's musical and spiritual experience leads to her guiding the youthful Santana (twenty-seven at the time, a decade younger than Coltrane). "Hanging around with Turiya inspired me to write some spiritual melodies, and when she heard them she surprised me by coming up with some arrangements to go along with them—symphonic oceans of sound. [...] Those first tunes became 'Angel of Air / Angel of Water' on the *Illuminations* album."[15] With Coltrane on harp and Santana playing guitar solos, the track is in complete contrast to "Angel of Sunlight."

"The engineer got an amazing tone on my guitar," recalls Santana of his first solo on "Angel of Sunlight," "partly because of the room but also because the [...] amplifier I brought with me had a second volume knob, which let me play softly but with a lot of intensity."[16] Despite finding this sonic tone, "my favorite moment on the whole album came right after I finished that solo. Suddenly Turiya blasted off like a spaceship, playing that Wurlitzer, bending the notes with her knees—she had some gizmo that stuck out of the side of the organ—and Jack [DeJohnette] and Dave [Holland] and I all looked at each other like we were hanging on for dear life! It was one of the most intense things I ever heard her play."[17] After the first few bars of the solo, DeJohnette increases the volume of his drumming and then Coster and Broussard solo on their Hammond organ and saxophone, respectively, continuing until the track reaches a mesmerizing climax.

Coltrane's fluid shift from piano to organ in the late 1960s was mirrored a few years later by her focus moving from organ to Wurlitzer. "In one meditation it was told to me that the organ had reached an age where it wouldn't serve properly [...] and the precise instrument I should get was revealed to me [...] and I could even read the insignia right there on the wood. So I went out to find the Wurlitzer."[18] *Universal Consciousness* (1971) may be the first LP by Coltrane to feature the Wurlitzer, but it comes into its own on "Angel of Sunlight," as if waiting for its sonic counterpoint with Santana's guitar. The Wurlitzer and amplifier are vital to the fusion of paths to reach the Universal Tone.

Despite the energy and passion behind *Illuminations*, sales were relatively poor and critical reception largely disparaging.[19] Perhaps in response to this, Santana immediately shifted toward a more scripted rock, typified by *Borboletta*, recorded just a few months later in 1974. Meanwhile, despite moving from Impulse! to the even more commercial Warner Brothers Records, Coltrane began to progressively retreat from the music business, becoming a Hindi swami in 1976 and eventually opening an ashram and retiring almost completely from the music business. Regardless of critical and commercial success, Coltrane and Santana instinctively sensed fusion was the only path through which music could develop. "That's how things change in music—one kind of music comes up next to another, and suddenly, shift!"[20] Their respective paths to the Universal Tone allow Coltrane and Santana's "Angel of Delight" to embody a significant, if overlooked, shift in the development of rock and jazz in the mid-1970s.

1. Carlos Santana, *The Universal Tone: Bringing My Story to Light* (London: Weidenfeld & Nicholson, 2014), 336.
2. See ibid., 267–68.
3. Ibid., 348.
4. Alice Coltrane, quoted in Edwin Pouncey, "Alice Coltrane: Enduring Love," *The Wire*, no. 218 (April 2002), www.thewire.co.uk/issues/218.
5. Santana, *The Universal Tone*, 197.
6. Ibid., 336.
7. Coltrane, quoted in Pouncey, "Alice Coltrane."
8. Alice Coltrane, quoted in Franya J. Berkman, "Universal Consciousness," in *Monument Eternal: The Music of Alice Coltrane* (Middletown, CT: Wesleyan University Press, 2010), 47.
9. Santana, *The Universal Tone*, 177.
10. Santana extended the path taken by the Byrds on tracks such as 1966's "Eight Miles High." See the interview with Roger McGuinn in J. C. Thomas, *Coltrane: Chasin' the Trane* (New York: Da Capo Press, 1976), 198–99.
11. Santana, *The Universal Tone*, 177.
12. Coltrane named one of his sons Ravi as a tribute to the sitar player after meeting him in the mid-'60s. At the time of Coltrane's death in 1967, the two were poised to work together. See Thomas, *Coltrane*, 199. For Shankar on Coltrane, see "Reminiscences about John Coltrane, 2001," https://www.ravishankar.org/reflections/reminiscences-about -john-coltrane-2001.
13. Santana, *The Universal Tone*, 365.
14. Alice Coltrane, quoted in Jimi Izrael, "Alice Coltrane, Wife of John, Left Her Own Mark" (January 16, 2007), NPR, https://www.npr.org /templates/story/story.php?storyId=6868236.
15. Santana, *The Universal Tone*, 365.
16. Ibid., 366.
17. Ibid.
18. Coltrane, quoted in Berkman, "Universal Consciousness," 80.
19. See Nick Kent, "Illuminations," *New Musical Express* (October 19, 1974).
20. Santana, *The Universal Tone*, 381.

4

Joni Mitchell and Wayne Shorter,
"Goodbye Pork Pie Hat" (1979)

Idioms

By working with composer and bassist Charles
Mingus and saxophonist Wayne Shorter on "Goodbye
Pork Pie Hat," Joni Mitchell fuses jazz and folk rock
by mixing idioms. With her voice and Shorter's
soprano saxophone running "out of phase," fusion
provides Mitchell with the tools to combat the narrow
confines of the mainstream rock world of the time.[1]

"Goodbye Pork Pie Hat" was originally composed by Mingus as an instrumental eulogy to saxophonist Lester Young, who died in 1959 (the "pork pie" being the horn player's signature style of hat). Twenty years later, the new version of the song is Mitchell's eulogy to Mingus, then at the end of his life. "I didn't want him to die before I finished 'Goodbye Pork Pie Hat,'" she says.[2] Despite the backstory, and being known for excelling at emotive vocal delivery, Mitchell's performance on the track feels emotionally cool.

Rather than grafting it from a track by Mingus, as would seem logical, Mitchell transfers the sonic dynamics underpinning "Goodbye Pork Pie Hat" from Miles Davis's "Nefertiti" (released in 1968, the same year as her first solo LP), a track highlighting the interplay between Shorter's saxophone and Davis's trumpet. "If you [...] listen to 'Nefertiti,' with Wayne Shorter and Miles playing, they start out in unison, but as the track goes on they pull away from each other. [...] They're still playing the same melody, but they're slightly out of phase with each other."[3] The saxophone and trumpet moving slightly "out of phase" in this way is felt acutely when you listen to the track. Replacing Davis's trumpet, Mitchell transposes this out-of-phase effect into "Goodbye Pork Pie Hat" by manipulating her voice as she scats, aping the sound of Shorter's soprano saxophone. Singers from the 1950s, such as Sarah Vaughan, frequently scatted but for a folk-rock singer of the 1970s to do so was unusual.

"Goodbye Pork Pie Hat" opens with stabbing notes from Jaco Pastorius's bass, offset by Shorter's soprano saxophone. Herbie Hancock alternates between playing short, choppy phrases and liquid runs on the Fender Rhodes that sweeten the track throughout. The lyrics set the stage in the first line of the first verse by recounting a conversation between Mitchell and Mingus: "When Charlie speaks of Lester / You know that someone great has gone." The remaining lines of the verse provide an insight into Young's struggles as an African American musician in a segregated America, "When the bandstand had a thousand ways / Of refusing a Black man admission." The second verse deals with the difficulties Young encountered in the 1940s when attempting to stay at hotels while in an interracial marriage: "When Lester took a wife / Arm and arm went black and white / And some saw red / And drove them from their bed." With Mitchell then being in a relationship with the African American percussionist Don Alias, these lyrics must have been particularly pertinent.

The lyrics change significantly in approach in the final verse. While "Charlie assailed me with historical information about Lester Young," explains Mitchell, "I still couldn't, with any conscience, simply write a historical song."[4] Attempting to pull the lyrics into the present and personalize them was a challenge. Inspiration hits one evening when she encounters a street scene in New York with Alias. The final verse of "Goodbye Pork Pie Hat" describes how "We came up from the subway / On the music midnight makes / To Charlie's bass and Lester's saxophone / In taxi horns and brakes." The contemporary urban scene is used to evoke Mingus and Young (the taxi horns perhaps sounding like a saxophone, and the brakes the double bass). "So the sidewalk leads us with music," sings Mitchell, fashioning a vignette describing two children dancing outside a bar, coincidentally called the Pork Pie Hat Bar.

"Goodbye Pork Pie Hat" and the entire *Mingus* (1979) project almost didn't happen due to the difficulties of fusing Mitchell's and Mingus's two very different idioms. Mingus's initial idea was to work with Mitchell on an interpretation of T. S. Eliot's *Four Quartets* (1941). The plan involved running two different types of music concurrently—one classical and another more urban—in the form of a duet between Mingus's bass notes and Mitchell's guitar. In Mingus's conception, two styles of vocals would accompany this: one a formal kind of voice speaking Eliot's words, the other a translation of it in vernacular English sung by Mitchell. But after reading the poems, Mitchell felt something as complex as Eliot's prose could not be condensed into lyrics fit for a popular song, and the idea was shelved. A month later, Mingus called Mitchell back with six new melodies titled "Joni 1," "Joni 2," and so on. Like the stories about Young, the melodies seemed to Mitchell to belong to the past, and she deemed them unsuitable. Balanced against this was "the very specialness of our relationship," reasons Mitchell, "[making] me think, 'Well, I'm gonna try this.'"[5] In an attempt to fuse their idioms, Mitchell and Mingus collaborate closely on each song's melody and arrangement. A sense of this closeness is portrayed in Mitchell's paintings used for the LP cover and insert, which depict Mitchell and Mingus deep in conversation.

While writing the lyrics to accompany the melodies, Mitchell asked Mingus to describe the moods suggested by each of the instrumental compositions. "The first one, he said, was, 'the things I'm going to miss,'" and "he looked at me and in that look I knew that [...] when you're confronted with the possible finality of [life], there are a million things you've left undone."[6] "So I simply became him in my imagination," Mitchell explains, and with the

track "Chair in the Sky" (originally titled "Joni 1")
"wrote [about] what he would miss."[7] Referring to
the jazz club in which Mingus frequently played in
the 1950s, one line in "Chair in the Sky" captures him
looking back: "In memories / Of old friends of mine /
In daydreams of Birdland / I see my soul on fire." The
remaining lines refer to other moments in his life.

Realizing more songs were needed to make the LP
full length, they rifled through Mingus's back catalog,
settling on "Goodbye Pork Pie Hat," first recorded in
1959. Crucially, Mitchell adapts her singing to Mingus's
melody lines. "It's melody with a lot of movement
to it," necessitating "a different kind of breathing.
And, ironically, it's a more natural form of music for
me as a singer than my own music because you have
such creative liberty within the bar."[8] The freedom of
movement these melodies afford Mitchell are key to
"Goodbye Pork Pie Hat" and the entire *Mingus* project.
"My instrument is better at a moderate volume," says
Mitchell of her voice, "using the dynamics of range,
phrasing and slurring and holding straight lines.
Like Miles."[9] So before even collaborating with jazz
musicians such as Mingus—and Pastorius, Shorter,
and Hancock—Mitchell perceived herself as sharing
interpretative and technical qualities with them.

With the melodies and lyrics now largely in place,
the instrumental treatment of the songs is next.
At Mingus's request, Mitchell recorded the songs at
New York's Electric Lady Studios with jazz musicians
Gerry Mulligan and Eddie Gómez playing acoustic
instruments. Although closer to what Mingus
wanted, "it just seemed tiring; all those solos" played
on traditional instruments, bemoans Mitchell.[10]
Introducing electric instruments, Mitchell eventually
finds a lineup and approach that works. Pastorius,

who first played electric bass for Mitchell on *Hejira* (1976), suggested Shorter play saxophone on her LP *Don Juan's Reckless Daughter* a year later. Weather Report's drummer Peter Erskine, accompanied by Alias on congas and Emil Richards on percussion, were the next to join. Hancock was the final addition. "When I got Herbie and Wayne from that Miles band, plus Jaco [Pastorius] and Peter from Weather Report, it wasn't all about solos anymore. Suddenly it was all about dialogues."[11] The new band decamps to A&M Studios in Los Angeles to cut the tracks, making music "so braided together that you couldn't take it apart."[12] The tightness is essential, enabling Mitchell and Shorter to play slightly "out of phase" with each other. Where some fusions between jazz and rock benefit from more exaggerated idiomatic dialogues, theirs is more subtle.

Despite the ingenuity of the other musicians, Shorter is Mitchell's key collaborator on "Goodbye Pork Pie Hat." After playing on Davis's "In a Silent Way" in early 1969, Shorter recorded his solo LP *Super Nova*, and then the first LP from Weather Report, the band he cofounded in 1971. From 1974, Shorter put his solo LPs on hold to make way for those by Weather Report; 1976's *Black Market* was the first to feature Pastorius. Mitchell and Shorter first work together in 1977 on a sixteen-minute episodic orchestral suite with a dreamy flashback section titled "Paprika Plains," destined for the LP *Don Juan's Daughter*. Listening to the track during a recording session in London, Shorter said, "Okay, Joni, this is like you're in Hyde Park after it rains and [...] there's a nanny with a baby in the boat on the pond, and her hand's just nudging the boat."[13] Mitchell was thrilled to have found someone able to create an impression of a scene in this way. "I don't think everyone is able to pick up on the pictograms [in Shorter's playing] because for a lot of people they just sound like dot dot dash. But those dot dot dashes are drawing an image to me."[14] Shorter also responded to the precise vocal inflections Mitchell produces for any given line. "There are places where I can tell he's touched by the tone in my vocal, 'cause he'll notice and respond to it, on one of the eleven takes. He'll never notice it again, because he'll be noticing something different in that spot on the next take."[15]

Throughout "Goodbye Pork Pie Hat," Mitchell constantly switches between being slightly in and out of phase with Shorter's soprano saxophone. When she delivers a line in a high register in the first verse ("A bright star in a dark age"), it's in phase with the saxophone, but with the next one they move slightly out. With the opening line of the second verse ("When Lester took a wife"), Mitchell sings deep within her chest, sounding more in unison with the bass, before tuning into the soprano saxophone in the verse's final phrases. While this play between voice and horn continues throughout the track, by far the purest interplay between the two comes when Mitchell scats. Following the third verse, after running at the same volume as Shorter, Mitchell's wordless voice gradually increases in presence, sustaining a note for countless bars as a saxophonist would. In Mitchell's words, this is where "the singer [is] imitating the horn" and "the horn is imitating the human voice."[16] Ultimately, the out-of-phase effect highlights the inherent awkwardness of the song, as Mitchell's voice and Shorter's saxophone sit uncomfortably next to one another and the other instruments, particularly Pastorius's busy bass. Reflected in its poor sales,

Mingus is surely the most difficult of Mitchell's LPs to enjoy due to the accentuation of these moments.[17]

Fusion affords Mitchell the freedom to innovate over time, finding her firmly resisting the tendency of the mainstream music business to keep contemporary jazz and folk rock separate: "[The] press didn't know what to do with the record so they either ignored it or treated it as some kind of breach of orthodoxy."[18] Mitchell's frustration is palpable, as the press "called [the LP] pretentious and [used] a lot of the kinds of adjectives that imply, 'Don't you know what you are?!'"[19] But Mitchell knew precisely who she was and which genres and idioms needed to be fused to articulate it. That the jazz world "allows you to grow old gracefully, whereas pop music is completely aligned with youth" also makes it attractive to a musician, then in her mid-thirties, whose moment of pop stardom had passed.[20] While jazz affords her creative freedom between 1975 and 1979, Mitchell is highly critical of the fad for jazz fusion prevalent in the 1970s. "Sometimes when producers push jazz in a fusion direction, they end up with a track that sounds like it's waiting for a singer," warns Mitchell.[21] Pursuing fusion as a process rather than a style, "Goodbye Pork Pie Hat" avoids this by using the out-of-phase effect to essay the tension between Mitchell and Mingus and their respective idioms.

1. Joni Mitchell, quoted in Vic Garbarini, "60 Minutes with Joni Mitchell," in *Joni on Joni: Interviews and Encounters with Joni Mitchell*, ed. Susan Whitall (Chicago, IL: Chicago Review Press, 2019), 199.
2. Joni Mitchell, quoted in David Yaffe, *Reckless Daughter: A Portrait of Joni Mitchell* (New York: Farrar, Straus and Giroux, 2017), 273.
3. Mitchell, quoted in Garbarini, "60 Minutes with Joni Mitchell," 199.
4. Joni Mitchell, quoted in Cameron Crowe, "Joni Mitchell Defends Herself" [1979], reprinted in *Joni on Joni*, 81.

5. Joni Mitchell, quoted in Malka Marom, *Joni Mitchell: Both Sides Now* (London: Omnibus Press, 2014), 133.

6. Joni Mitchell, quoted in Ben Sidran, "The Underdog Meets Joni Mitchell: Charles Mingus Finds a New Voice" [1978], reprinted in *Reckless Daughter: A Joni Mitchell Anthology*, ed. Barney Hoskyns (London: Constable, 2016), 131.

7. Ibid.

8. Ibid., 132.

9. Ibid., 133.

10. Joni Mitchell, quoted in Geoffrey Himes, "Music and Lyrics," in *Joni on Joni*, 337. These may be released as part of the ongoing Joni Mitchell Archives project.

11. Mitchell, quoted in Himes, "Music and Lyrics," 337.

12. Joni Mitchell, quoted in Nick Hasted, "Mingus," *Uncut* (December 2020), https://jonimitchell.com/library/view.cfm?id=5049.

13. Joni Mitchell, quoted in Michelle Mercer, *Footprints: The Life and Work of Wayne Shorter* (New York: Penguin, 2007), 200.

14. Ibid., 202.

15. Ibid., 201–202.

16. Mitchell, quoted in Sidran, "The Underdog Meets Joni Mitchell," 132.

17. By no coincidence, Mitchell's next LP, 1982's *Wild Things Run Fast*, returns to the rock instrumentation and song length of 1974's *Court and Spark*, her last (and most popular) studio LP before the jazz-inflected series that started with 1975's *The Hissing of Summer Lawns* and culminated in *Mingus*.

18. Joni Mitchell, quoted in Kristine McKenna, "The Dream Girl Wakes Up" [1982], reprinted in *Reckless Daughter*, ed. Hoskyns, 146.

19. Ibid.

20. Ibid., 149.

21. Mitchell, quoted in Mercer, *Footprints*, 219.

5

Kimiko Kasai and Herbie Hancock, "Butterfly" (1979)

East/West

Japanese vocalist Kimiko Kasai and Herbie Hancock collaborate to fuse funk and jazz on "Butterfly," recorded in Tokyo in 1979, uniting Eastern and Western musical cultures. On the track, Kasai and Hancock manipulate vibrato using their respective instruments, the voice and the Fender Rhodes.

As "Butterfly" starts, the liquid run of notes coming from Hancock's keyboard bounce from the left and then the right of the soundstage. A beat on a tom-tom follows and then comes the ping of an electric bass. Gradually, all three instruments increase in volume and Kasai enters with the first words ("Precious day"), projecting the word "day" forward. With the keyboard riff from the opening bars continuing, focus flits between Kasai's vibrato and the ripple of Hancock's Fender Rhodes. Seeming to mimic the way Hancock's electric keyboard modulates the pitch of a note, on the word "sun" from the second line ("You're the sun") Kasai's voice wavers exaggeratedly as it moves between sharp and flat.

The path to recording "Butterfly" for both musicians is a circuitous one. Kasai's 1968 debut LP is a collaboration with pianist Yuzuru Sera, followed two years later by a live solo album. Then, backed by the Kosuke Mine Quartet, Kasai refines her movement between smoky midrange and extended upper-range vocals with 1971's *Yellow Carcass in the Blue*, before collaborating with two other major figures of Western jazz: Gil Evans in 1972 and Teo Macero in 1975 and 1976. A harbinger of their forthcoming full-length collaboration, in 1978 Kasai records Hancock's "Chameleon" for her solo LP *Round and Round*, with Hancock playing the same squelchy synthesizer sound featured on the instrumental original (from 1973's *Head Hunters* LP).

Jazz's fusion with funk was going at full tilt in North America in the 1970s, and Japan was enjoying a similar wave of activity, heightened in the mid-1970s by the likes of Ryo Kawasaki's *Juice* (1976). Underpinning contemporary Japanese jazz is the influence of Hancock's funk-laced LPs *Thrust* (1974) and *Man-Child* (1975) (which incorporated aspects of Sly and the Family Stone's sound). Facilitating this dialogue,

Sony develops a long-standing relationship with Columbia Records—Hancock's label—and eventually acquired it in the 1980s. Spotlighting the primacy of Japan's role in the global economy, the cofounder of Sony, Morita Akio, later cowrites the book *The Japan That Can Say No: Why Japan Will Be the First Among Equals* as a riposte to President Carter's claim at a G7 summit meeting held in Tokyo in 1979 (the same year as the release of *Butterfly*) that US-Japan relations were mutually advantageous.[1]

By mimicking each other's modulation of vibrato, Kasai and Hancock's collaboration subtly reflects this push and pull between the two nations.[2] Kazumi Kurigami's cover photography and art direction for the LP visually plays up this dynamic by using a saturated image of Kasai's head and shoulders that echoes Andy Warhol's portraits. Even though the typography on the cover mentions Hancock (and he is pictured on the insert), with the LP being recorded, produced, designed, and released in Japan, it gives the sense that it's a Kasai solo LP rather than a collaboration.

The North American jazz vocalist Chris Connor is crucial to the formation of Kasai's vocal character. "I was thirteen, studying at home in Kyoto, when I heard Chris Connor's 'All About Ronnie' on the radio," Kasai remembers; "it felt like an electric shock."[3] Taken from 1954's *Chris Connor Sings Lullabys of Birdland*, the track features Connor's trademark smoky voice frequently stretching into the upper register. While other jazz singers of the era excel at smoky midrange vocals, few have such a well-developed upper register as Connor. Two years later, on "Where Are You?" Connor extends her vocal range further, using the slower pace of the track as an opportunity to endlessly stretch words and phrases out. Kasai lifts Connor's ability to hit an incredibly high note and modulate it, but makes it her own.

When Kasai sings in English on earlier LPs, including those with Evans and Macero, it sounds as though she is mimicking a North American singing voice, which limits her vocal range (as she hits no exaggerated high notes whatsoever). Before "Butterfly," Kasai channels Connor only when singing in her native tongue, like on the ballad "Yarikake No Jinsei" from 1977's *Tokyo Special*, where her voice displays an incredible degree of modulated vibrato. On "Butterfly" Kasai uses the voice showcased on "Yarikake No Jinsei" while singing in English for the first time, subtly fusing Eastern and Western sensibilities and playing through the bilingual versatility of earlier Japanese vocalists from the Ryūkōka genre of popular song.

Along with Kasai's voice, the central instrument on "Butterfly" is the Fender Rhodes, a keyboard Hancock was introduced to by Miles Davis during the recording of "Stuff" for 1968's *Miles in the Sky*. Davis was made aware of the Fender Rhodes as early as 1966, a year after the instrument became commercially available, leading him to press the instrument onto Hancock: "I walked into the studio and there was no piano for me to play. [...] I finally said, 'Miles, what am I supposed to play?' 'Play that,' he said, and nodded toward a Fender Rhodes electric piano in the corner. [...] I walked over, flipped it on, and played a chord. And, to my surprise, I thought it sounded kind of cool."[4]

In less than two years, the Fender Rhodes proved to be indispensable to Hancock. Attempts to further broaden the range of sounds by jury-rigging effects pedals to the Fender Rhodes—including a wah-wah and an Echoplex—eventually lead Hancock to embrace the synthesizer, an instrument with the capability to produce all these effects and more. Featuring sci-fi-like sonic swooshes, "Quasar" from 1972's *Crossings* is Hancock's first track to use the synthesizer. "What I heard was so hip and majestic, it was just fantastic. [The] synthesizer added a phenomenal new element to the music."[5] On *Thrust* Hancock weaves the synthesizer even more forcefully into his funk-driven sound.

Familiarity with the synthesizer takes Hancock to the vocoder, a device for scrambling and encoding speech communication developed in 1928 and first demonstrated in 1939 in New York World's Fair.[6] The vocoder is a black box with inputs to plug in synthesizers, keyboards, and microphones. Hancock immediately began thinking of ways to use the device, and his technical team configured the vocoder to sound human enough to be used on a lead vocal. Without the experience of producing the vocoder-driven tracks on *Sunlight* (1978), Hancock may not have developed such an acute sensitivity to Kasai's voice a year later. (In 2022, Hancock reprises his use of the vocoder on a track from Domi and JD Beck's LP *Not Tight*.)

Experimenting with the vocoder while recording *Sunlight*, Hancock realizes that "the vibrato in a singing voice is actually three kinds of vibrato—the modulation of volume, pitch, and filter."[7] Serving as a type of translation device for the duo, the vocoder is fundamental to Hancock's understanding of Kasai's voice. Typified by "I Thought It Was You," other tracks on *Butterfly* merge Kasai's voice and the vocoder, as if theorist Donna Haraway's soon-to-be published analysis of cyborgian women in technoscience is sonically put into practice. Soon, the vocoder becomes popularized by the likes of Laurie Anderson, with *Big Science* (1982), but Kasai and Hancock subtly play through Haraway's logic three years earlier.

Butterfly is distinctive as it marks the first time Hancock collaborates with a vocalist on every track of an LP. If Hancock's funk-laced jazz informs Kasai up to this point, then Kasai's vocal character and city-pop sound become crucial to the next stage of Hancock's development. Prototyped in the mid-1970s by the likes of Yumi Matsutoya, city pop is a slick, urban type of technology-laced pop music. Following *Butterfly*, Hancock veers away from funk-based jazz toward his own version of city pop—a move started with the vocoder-saturated tracks on *Sunlight* but intensified after the collaborative LP with Kasai in 1979. His 1980 LP *Monster* features vocals without the vocoder on every track, and is followed by *Magic Windows* a year later. This moment between the classic funk LPs of the 1970s and the techno-pop of the mid-1980s (including *Future Shock*) is unjustly overlooked within Hancock's discography, obfuscating the impact of Kasai on him.

The collaboration between Kasai and Hancock on "Butterfly" is situated within their work with the other musicians on the track, including keyboard player Webster Lewis, drummer Alphonse Mouzon, guitarist Ray Obiedo, multireed player Bennie Maupin, and bassist Paul Jackson (the latter two part of Hancock's the Headhunters). In the first part of "Butterfly" when Kasai and Hancock emphasize a phrase ("Rest your wings") by pausing for a beat, cabaret style, the tightness of the interplay between the duo and the other musicians is heightened. In the second half of "Butterfly" the exchange between Maupin and Jackson becomes central, with the rest of the track featuring a delicate interplay between the instruments before Kasai returns for a final verse and chorus.

"Butterfly" takes Kasai and Hancock further away from stricter definitions of jazz. "The fact that I was playing so many different kinds of electronic instruments definitely irritated some jazz purists," writes Hancock. "They feared that with so many musicians branching out into fusion and other genres, classic jazz was in danger of dying out."[8] Underlining the way Hancock conceived of fusion as a process rather than a style, Hancock writes of how once 1973's *Head Hunters* LP "wound up with a jazz fusion label on it," jazz's fusion with funk had become somewhat "shallow and stereotypical."[9] With the turn into the 1980s, Hancock and Kasai both leave jazz's fusion with funk behind to embrace jazz's fusion with pop, bringing Kasai to 1982's *Kimiko* and Hancock to the biggest hit of his career, 1983's "Rockit." The fusion their collaboration in 1979 triggered is essential to both musicians' ability to take part in shaping the sound of the following decade.

1. See Nicholas Bayne and Robert D. Putnam, *Hanging in There: The G7 and G8 Summit in Maturity and Renewal* (Aldershot: Ashgate Publishing, 2000).
2. See Loren Kajikawa, "The Sound of Struggle: Black Revolutionary Nationalism and Asian American Jazz," in *Jazz/Not Jazz: The Music and Its Boundaries*, ed. David Ake, Charles Hiroshi Garrett, and Daniel Goldmark (Berkeley, CA: University of California Press, 2012), 190–216.
3. Kimiko Kasai, "Interview/Kimiko Kasai," trans. Rami Suzuki, *Ban Ban Ton Ton* (May 20, 2018), https://banbantonton.com/2018/05/20/interview-kimiko-kasai/.
4. Herbie Hancock, *Possibilities* (London: Penguin Books, 2014), 103–104.
5. Ibid., 145.
6. Ibid., 210.
7. Ibid., 212.
8. Ibid., 221.

9. Ibid. For an in-depth analysis of this LP, see Steven F. Pond, *Head Hunters: The Making of Jazz's First Platinum Album* (Ann Arbor, MI: University of Michigan Press, 2005).

6

Lou Reed and Don Cherry, "The Bells" (1979)

Philosophies

"The Bells" fuses the instrumentation of alternative
rock with the compositional and improvisational
techniques of free jazz. Producing a sound Lou
Reed refers to as "dissonant," the fusion of genres
on "The Bells" flows from his and Don Cherry's
complementary philosophies.[1] On "The Bells" Reed
extends the Velvet Underground's earlier pursuit
of improvisation by collaborating with Cherry,

one of their inspirations and a leading proponent of free jazz. Where fusion enables Reed to tap into his emotional intelligence, it provides Cherry with the means to embrace the contemporary in the guise of post-punk.

The collaboration is crucial to both musicians, propelling Reed beyond the nihilistic themes occupying him lyrically for much of the 1970s and pushing Cherry past the comfort of the New Age spirituality absorbing him from the late 1960s onward. As a result of their collaboration, the song is one of the most challenging fusions of rock and jazz in a year full of them. "There's a real band on this record," opined Lester Bangs in *Rolling Stone*, "and these musicians are giving us the only true jazz-rock fusion anybody's come up with since Miles Davis's *On the Corner* period."[2]

Throughout the gruelling nine minutes of "The Bells," Reed's synthesized guitar and Cherry's pocket trumpet tussle for primacy. The track builds slowly, with Reed attempting to push against Cherry's trumpet with a wall of synthesized guitar for over half its length. The dissonance becomes exaggerated when Reed's voice enters after five-and-a-half minutes. Accurately characterized by one commentator as sounding "like the heat-howl of the dying otter,"[3] Reed's voice delivers the opening couplet: "And the actresses relate / To the actor who comes home late." The lyrics detail the impression the song's protagonist has of Broadway while standing on the precipice of a tall building just before jumping off. They climax with the emphatic phrase, "And he sang out, 'Here come the bells! / Here come the bells!'" A chorus of voices join Reed as the phrase is repeated; there's a slight reprisal of synthesized guitar, a final blast from Cherry's horn, and the track ends. Due to the oddness of its structure—the usual verse/chorus alternation of rock is usurped—and the dirge-like sound of the synthesized guitar as it presses against the trumpet, it takes countless listens to find a way into "The Bells."

By pursuing the collaboration with Cherry, Reed sets out to deliberately fuse alternative rock and free jazz. "I liked Ornette Coleman a lot, and Don Cherry a whole lot," recalls Reed, "I used to always go see 'em at clubs."[4] The feeling was mutual. "Lou Reed: I always had the greatest respect for him [...] because his poetry is the poetry of the street."[5] The experience of listening to Coleman's and Cherry's free jazz was formative to Reed's entire approach to the Velvet Underground's longer experimental tracks recorded in 1966 and 1967. "I'd had this idea [...]: wouldn't it be incredible if you could play like Ornette Coleman on the guitar?"[6]

Ceasing to be a regular member of Coleman's quartet, Cherry develops his own sound—with the release of his solo debut LP, 1966's *Complete Communion*, and two further LPs on Blue Note. Reed takes a parallel route vis-à-vis the Velvet Underground. But with the turn into the 1970s, Reed and Cherry eschew sonic dissonance in favor of the melodic and the ambient: Reed's debut LP released in 1972 is packed full of sweet melodies, and 1970's *Mu (Second Part)* finds Cherry exploring the spiritual by incorporating aspects of the ambient culled from non-Western music.

In the late 1960s, Cherry gradually relocates from New York to the village of Tågarp, Sweden, to establish a collective workshop in an abandoned schoolhouse, collaborating with both his partner, the textile artist Moki Cherry, and visiting musicians. Cherry's collaboration with Reed is a continuation of this process, and one that greatly impacts the trumpeter, informing the direction he pursues next. Following "The Bells," Cherry embraces punk rock by touring with the Slits later in 1979, playing on Ian Dury's *Laughter* in 1980, and on Rip Rig + Panic's *I Am Cold* (featuring stepdaughter Neneh Cherry) two years later.

Meanwhile, in 1979 Reed finally moves away from the nihilism of *Berlin* (1973), an LP charting the rise and fall of a relationship with its conclusion in suicide, and 1978's *Street Hassle*, with the put-down song "Dirt" aimed at his manager. Besides the title track, *The Bells* also includes reflections on the need for redemption ("All Through the Night"), family ("Families"), and the desire to be loved ("Looking for Love"). Reed's next LP, 1980's *Growing Up in Public*, pushes even further into this emotive territory with reflections on romance, the complexity of parental relationships, and male shyness. This shift in sensibility reconnects Reed with the more tender emotions explored on two of the Velvet Underground's LPs largely overlooked by post-punk: the self-titled, third LP released in 1969 (including "I'm Set Free") and 1970's *Loaded* (featuring "New Age").[7] That is, for three years between 1969 and 1971, Reed pursues a very different direction to the one he is most associated with. From the time of recording "The Bells" onward, Reed's emotional intelligence comes to the fore again, suggesting the impact of the collaboration with Cherry is both immediate and long-reaching.

The backstory to their collaboration on "The Bells" begins three years earlier with a chance encounter. Reed's saxophone player Marty Fogel bumped into

Cherry in November 1976 at Los Angeles airport (after first meeting in New York as his rehearsal space was next door to Moki Cherry's workshop). "We were getting ready to go, and I said to Lou, 'Man, I just ran into Don Cherry out there!' He says, 'Go get him! Go get him! I love him!'"[8] Reed then invited Cherry to join his live band for two dates, playing on Velvet Underground classics as well as new songs—without any prior rehearsal. Bootlegs from one of the shows reveal how Cherry accentuates the band's existing improvisational elements. Where the LP version of "Coney Island Baby" is six-and-a-half minutes long, the live version stretches out for over nine minutes, with Cherry clearly audible during the quieter passages, playing a particularly memorable solo behind Fogel's saxophone at just over four minutes in. The contrast between the studio and live versions of "Charley's Girl" is even more extreme, with the former lasting for two-and-a-half minutes and the latter clocking in at a whopping twelve minutes. Cherry's solos become more independent and inventive, the trumpet battling against the distorted guitar and keyboards. Cherry intrigued Reed's keyboard player Michael Fonfara. "Don Cherry is positively spiritual onstage. He'd suddenly come creeping in from between the amplifiers [...] like an apparition [...] and then he'd hit two or three notes," lending "a lot of meaning to what Lou was saying."[9]

A three-year intermission follows. During this period, they each release only one studio LP, Cherry's *Here & Now* in 1977 and Reed's *Street Hassle* in 1978, and then early in 1979 Reed invites Cherry to collaborate on *The Bells*. Cherry composes "All Through the Night" with Reed and coarranges "With You," but the title track is easily the most compelling result of their collaboration on the LP, generating sonic dissonance by adopting the approach of free jazz within the context of alternative rock. "I was in the studio one night late, just playing the piano and playing part of 'The Bells' that I had composed," Fonfara remembers, "and Reed came into the studio and said, 'What's that?' and I explained it to him. And he said, 'I want to record that.'"[10] They cut the track and Reed improvised the lyrics. "The Bells" was "constructed in the studio, and sung one time and one time only."[11] The lyrics are as improvised as the instrumentation. Referencing this, Cherry claimed "the musician-artist should be a master of improvising," as they "put a lot of value on bringing the music alive" by "playing together."[12]

As the electric guitar is Reed's main instrument, so the acoustic pocket trumpet is Cherry's. "The first [trumpet] I had was made in Pakistan and that was in the '50s when I first started playing with Ornette," Cherry notes, and being "a very thin, small [person] it gets right to my nature, and I can hear [it] instantly because of it not being too long."[13] (The pocket trumpet uses the same amount of tubing as a regular trumpet except that it's curled around more tightly.) Where Cherry seeks proximity with the analog vibrations of his instrument, it's as if Reed consciously introduces distance, going one step beyond the Guitarman plexiglass electric guitar he routinely used in the late 1970s by turning to the newly released Roland guitar synthesizer, an instrument introducing a broad spectrum of sonic textures into the palette of the six-string guitar. The dissonant sounds their fusion on "The Bells" generates are the result of their respective approaches to their instruments. Featuring a grainy black-and-white portrait by Garry

Cross of Reed holding a mirror, the LP cover for *The Bells* makes no attempt to convey the nature of the music on the LP. With Cherry's name hidden in a list of credits on the insert, there's the sense that Arista Records — and Reed too? — insisted on it being positioned as a solo LP.

The fusion the collaboration between Reed and Cherry triggered is set within the broader fusion between jazz and alternative rock already taking place within Reed's studio band. In 1979 this includes progressive rock keyboard player Michael Fonfara, soprano and tenor saxophonist Marty Fogel, rock percussionist Michael Suchorsky, and blues bass player Ellard-James Boles. Reed and Cherry may be the focal points on "The Bells," but the rest of the band are fundamental to fulfilling its sound; Cherry even uses Reed's band later in 1979 when touring with the Slits. (With the recent interest in Cherry shown by magazines such as *The Wire* — their September 2023 issue features numerous newly commissioned articles on him — and Blank Forms releasing rare sessions and concerts, this aspect of his output will hopefully soon be brought into crisper focus.)

Reed is reflective about the deeper history of the exchange between jazz and rock. "I read that [Ornette Coleman] played in Little Richard's band [...] I mean it's interesting the crossover that goes on there, you can hear it on 'Ramblin.' It's just POW!"[14] Though not substantiated by Coleman's biographers, Reed's fascination alone with the anecdote is telling.[15] The history of the fusion between jazz and rock that Reed perceives to be in motion in Coleman's output leads to his making a special request when cutting "The Bells": "Don Cherry knows how I love that line [...] in [Coleman's] 'Lonely Woman,' and I just asked him if he'd put it in 'The Bells.' And he quotes that line in the intro."[16] The line is barely audible on the finished track, but it's there.

While Reed firmly places himself in the métier of rock—the autobiographic lyrics to 1970's "Rock and Roll" describe the life of the song's protagonist as being saved by it—Cherry is not so comfortable doing so with jazz. Pressed by an interviewer to define his music in terms of genre, a frustrated Cherry replies: "if you put a label on it like jazz" then "that's canning it."[17] Cherry describes how free jazz "really lives because you can see there is no time period," whereas "style is only related to a certain period."[18] While Cherry expands the remit of jazz in the late 1960s and into the 1970s, for the most part it is not via a fusion with rock (only embracing the electric guitar on studio LPs occasionally) but the rhythms of Middle Eastern music.

Foreshadowing Moor Mother's later fusion of rap and free jazz—Reed's spoken-word delivery of lyrics devoted to urban themes is a form of proto-rap in line with Gil Scott-Heron's work—"The Bells" is an overlooked but compelling example of fusion as process. At a fundamental moment in their creative development, the way the fusion of philosophies drives the fusion of genres empowers Reed to foreground his emotional intelligence and Cherry to embrace the contemporary.

1. Lou Reed, quoted in David Fricke, "Lou Reed: The Rolling Stone Interview," *Rolling Stone* (May 4, 1989), https://www.rollingstone.com/music/music-news/lou-reed-therolling-stone-interview-2-174015/.

2. Lester Bangs, "The Bells," *Rolling Stone* (June 14, 1979), https://www.rollingstone.com/music/music-album-reviews/the-bells-192254/. Also see Greil Marcus's review of the LP, *Village Voice* (May 1979), https://greilmarcus.net/2014/11/11/lou-reed-the-bells-0579/.

3. Roger Klorese, quoted in Diana Clapton, *Lou Reed & The Velvet Underground* (London: Bobcat Books, 1987), 56.

4. Lou Reed, quoted in Dave DiMartino, "The Power of Positive Pinball: Lou Reed Tilts the Machine," *CREEM* [September 1980], reprinted in Pat Thomas, ed., *My Week Beats Your Year: Encounters with Lou Reed* (Los Angeles, CA: Hat & Beard Press, 2018), 187. Reed collaborated with Ornette Coleman on the track "Guilty" on *The Raven* (Sire Records, 2003).

5. Don Cherry, quoted in Ben Sidran, "Don Cherry Talking Jazz" (December 14, 1986), https://bensidran.com/conversation/talking-jazz-don-cherry.

6. Reed, quoted in DiMartino, "The Power of Positive Pinball," 187.

7. Patti Smith was one of the few punk musicians drawn precisely to the band's third LP, frequently covering "Pale Blue Eyes" in concert from 1976 onward.

8. Marty Fogel, quoted in Aidan Levy, "Rock & Roll & Free Jazz: Inside Lou Reed and Don Cherry's Avant-Fusion," *Jazz Times* (April 25, 2019).

9. Michael Fonfara, quoted in Anthony DeCurtis, *Lou Reed: A Life* (London: John Murray, 2017), 250.

10. Fonfara, quoted in Levy, "Rock & Roll & Free Jazz."

11. Lou Reed, quoted in Mick Wall, *Lou Reed: The Life* (London: Orion, 2013), 178.

12. Don Cherry, quoted in Amiri Baraka, "Don Cherry" [1963], in *Black Music* (New York: Akashic, 2010), 165.

13. Don Cherry, quoted in Terry Gross, "Remembering Don Cherry," *Fresh Air* (October 24, 1995), https://freshairarchive.org/segments/remembering-don-cherry.

14. Reed, quoted in Di Martino, "The Power of Positive Pinball," 187.

15. See the authoritative biography by Maria Golia, *Ornette Coleman: The Territory and the Adventure* (London: Reaktion Books, 2020).

16. Ibid.

17. Don Cherry, quoted in Arthur Taylor, "Don Cherry," in *Notes and Tones: Musician-to-Musician Interviews* (New York: Da Capo Press, 1993), 177.

18. Don Cherry, quoted in Valerie Wilmer, "Ornette Coleman – The Art of the Improvisor," in *As Serious as Your Life: Black Music and the Free Jazz Revolution, 1957–1977* (London: Serpent's Tail, 2018), 80.

7

Lora Logic and Lora Logic, "Brute Fury" (1982)

Sensibilities

By fusing high-pitched vocals and frenetic tenor saxophone, "Brute Fury" from Lora Logic's only solo LP *Pedigree Charm* (1982) creates an unlikely fusion between post-punk and free jazz. The track is defined by a clash of sensibilities, leading to a sonic effect Logic describes as "Dadaistic," lending her a distinct sense of identity that was essential to securing a place within the music scene of the time.[1]

"Brute Fury" opens with a circular saxophone riff, double-tracked and panned to either side of the sound stage, lending the interplay an exaggerated spatial dynamic. Once the saxophone introduction ends, the main body of the song kicks in. A propulsive rhythm guitar accompanies a galloping drumbeat for several bars, until Logic's crystal-clear voice enters. As she replies to the play on the title phrase ("Fury / Brute Fury") with the line "They couldn't find the answers," the saxophone reenters, bordering on the atonal as the double-tracked instrument vies for space alongside the double-tracked voice. Their collision continues, off and on, for the rest of the track, suffusing the listener in a flurry of high-pitched treble notes. On "Brute Fury," Logic the saxophone player collaborates with Logic the singer.

Highlighted by an emphasis on the trill— a rapid alternation of notes producing a quavering sound—the relationship between Logic's voice and saxophone playing is central to the way "Brute Fury" fuses genres and sensibilities. Where Joni Mitchell's fusion of jazz and folk rock on 1979's "Goodbye Pork Pie Hat" features Wayne Shorter playing the soprano saxophone while she sings, on "Brute Fury" Logic assumes both roles, giving her an incredible degree of control as she clashes the two together in Dadaistic fashion.[2] "One of the reasons I liked the saxophone," Logic says, "is because it sounded like the human voice; there's something very warm and emotional about it, and its effect on the human ear is very similar."[3] In an April 1982 article coinciding with the release of *Pedigree Charm*, jazz critic Richard Cook pinpoints the relationship Logic established between her voice and saxophone playing, describing how the latter "is openly speech-like in its expressivity."[4]

Logic's personification of her voice on saxophone is central to the way genres and sensibilities fuse on "Brute Fury."

Growing up in northwest London, Logic turned to the tenor saxophone in her early teens, attending lessons in nearby Willesden Green. "Once I got over the physical challenge of producing enough breath and my lips not being sore," she remembers, "I'd play saxophone for five hours a day."[5] Bored of blowing along to records at home, in 1976 Logic responded to an advertisement in music paper the *Melody Maker* to join the punk band X-Ray Spex, led by vocalist Poly Styrene. Besides appearing on their debut single, "Oh Bondage Up Yours!" (1977), Logic composed the saxophone arrangements for X-Ray Spex's debut LP *Germfree Adolescents*, released a year later. But with Poly Styrene not willing to share the spotlight, Logic was ejected from the band prior to recording her parts.

The decision to then front her own band, Essential Logic, forced Logic to extend her remit beyond the saxophone. "Singing was not something I really thought about, especially at the beginning," but it was essential to leading a band.[6] Released in 1979, the single "Aerosol Burns" is Logic's first attempt at a vocal, using an aggressive high-pitched attack not unlike Poly Styrene. Other tracks on Essential Logic's debut LP *Beat Rhythm News*, such as "Quality Cray Wax O.K." and "Shabby Abbott," feature Logic experimenting with a voice somewhere in the midrange, while the saxophone parts frequently obliterate her singing.

Logic's next LP features a more complimentary interplay between the saxophone and voice. "Because the music on *Pedigree Charm* was more complex than *Beat Rhythm News*, I heard a more

delicate voice with all kinds of harmonies."[7] A Peel
Session in 1981 featuring the title track together
with "Martian Man" and "Rat Alley" captures Logic
in a period of transition between 1979's *Beat Rhythm
News* and 1982's *Pedigree Charm*; the roughness is
still there, but a more complex musical vocabulary
is just beginning to appear. A year later, the debut LP
contains an incredible range of singing and saxophone
playing, the voice and instrument carefully tuned
to one another. Alternating between the melody
and harmony, "Horrible Party" reveals Logic's subtle
vocal shadings, while "Martian Man" blends carefully
pitched multiple-tracked voices together. The
way Logic's saxophone playing intersects with her
singing is also more complementary with "Stop Halt"
using a lower register of notes to play underneath
the voice, and "Pedigree Charm" nimbly injecting
sharp saxophone phrases in between vocal passages.
With the appearance of other bands such as Rip Rig +
Panic on the scene in the early 1980s, the fusion of
free jazz and post-punk began gaining ground in the
United Kingdom (as it had a few years earlier in North
America with James Chance and the Contortions).

Logic's reference to the clash of sensibilities
taking place in her music as being "Dadaistic"
is well founded. Cultivating spontaneity, in the
1920s Dada artists used the abrasive meeting of
dissimilar elements the medium of collage provides
to combat established aesthetic and social norms.
Reflected in the designs for their covers, punk and
post-punk bands such as Siouxsie and the Banshees
frequently cited Dada as a key reference.[8] If the
tracks on *Beat Rhythm News* were redolent of the
extreme juxtaposition of visual elements common
to Dada, then *Pedigree Charm* activates them in

a relatively nuanced way. The clash the fusion of genres and sensibilities creates is still there in 1982 but it's gentler. The covers to both LPs emphasize this: while Zut Graphics used an angular montage of monochrome surfaces and type for *Beat Rhythm News*, Martyn Lambert floats an elegant linear illustration of Logic's head over a colorfully flecked background for *Pedigree Charm*.

The lyrics to "Brute Fury" extend the quest for individuality driving Logic's singing and playing. Logic admits that "words always come first for me. I put the music around them. I write things down all the time. Most rock music has a vocabulary of twenty words which is just used over and over again. What's interesting about modern music is that you should be able to say more."[9] The lyrics to "Brute Fury" do precisely this by critiquing the lifestyle of her parents: "Mummy has a temper, a temper, a temper / Daddy has a headache / If only they'd been stronger, and wiser, and calmer." "They're about seeing my parents working their whole lives just to get a roof over their heads and not wanting to end up in that story."[10] Reinforced by the clash of sensibilities generated by the fusion of post-punk and free jazz, the lyrics to "Brute Fury" succinctly capture Logic's exasperation.

The track's other musicians—Charlie Haywood on drums, Ben Annesley on bass, and Phil Legg on guitar—are essential to its fusion of free jazz and post-punk. "When Charlie Haywood started playing his drums I responded. It was so inspiring to hear him, I just improvised, producing layers on layers of sound. Something like the beginning of 'Brute Fury,' is obviously arranged but after that initial layer the sax is all improvised."[11] Although it sounds like the obverse is the case due to its increased level of complexity, "*Pedigree Charm* is more spontaneous," explains Logic, "because we hadn't played the songs endlessly on the road."[12] Similarly, the precision of Logic's own playing is not wrought from daily practice: "It's risky [not practicing], I suppose [but] I quite like that" since "I never wanted to be a great player or singer. Just good enough to translate what I want."[13] The song's producer, Phil Legg, who later would go on to work with more mainstream artists who fused jazz (such as Sade), works in an improvisational way too. Legg, who also played guitar, "was so devoted to that album. It was his first record [and he] taught himself while we were making it; we had an eight-track tape recorder in the squat and took it to a studio in Brixton and Phil put that album together with the eight track and a simple mixing desk."[14] Listening to "Brute Fury" on headphones, especially the remastered vinyl released in 2024, it is clearly audible that the different vocal and saxophone tracks drop in and out in a loose fashion. With the spontaneous clash of elements running right through from the musicians to the producer, the fusion of sensibilities and genres on "Brute Fury" conveys a compelling sense of freedom and individuality.

In Dadaist fashion, a disregard for conventional genres underpins Logic's approach to fusing free jazz and post-punk. "I'd never thought about categories, it just never occurred to me. [...] We were on Rough Trade and were encouraged to be ourselves and make the music that we wanted. There weren't many filtering processes or boundaries. I never thought while I was making *Pedigree Charm* 'now it's becoming more jazzy.'"[15] While Logic confesses to having little knowledge of free-jazz musicians like Don Cherry at the time, the trumpeter knew of Essential Logic, revealed during an interview in which he exclaims, "I love the way she sticks with it!" — referring to a prolonged saxophone and vocal riff.[16] Logic is drawn more to the playing of Bill Haley's saxophonist Rudy Pompilli due to what she characterizes as his "simple, punchy riffs," as per tracks on *Rockin' the Joint* (1958).[17] While the saxophone phrasing on "Brute Fury" sounds close to Pompilli's playing, Logic's Dadaistic play of vocal and saxophone tones feels nearer to the way Cherry's horn clashes with Ornette Coleman on his LP *Something Else!!!!*, released the same year as Haley's, in 1958. Current accounts of post-punk may continue to downplay her role, but Logic's fusion of genres by fusing sensibilities makes her voice vital to the era.[18]

1. "Lora Logic: The John Robb Interview" (February 17, 2023), https://www.youtube.com/watch?v=Q5K8yuvN2KE.
2. Joni Mitchell, quoted in Vic Garbarini, "60 Minutes with Joni Mitchell," in *Joni on Joni: Interviews and Encounters with Joni Mitchell*, ed. Susan Whitall (Chicago, IL: Chicago Review Press, 2019), 199.
3. Lora Logic, interview with the author, December 2023.
4. Richard Cook, "The Essentially Perilous Logic of Lora," *NME* (April 3, 1982): 17. Also see Greil Marcus, "Fanfare in the Garden," liner notes, Lora Logic, *Essential Logic: Fanfare in the Garden* (Kill Rock Stars, 2003), https://greilmarcus.net/2014/08/26/essential -logic-fanfare-in-the-garden-2003/.
5. Lora Logic, quoted in Stevie Chick, "Interview with Lora Logic," *Guardian* (November 28, 2022), https://www.theguardian.com /music/2022/nov/28/id-wear-a-mac-on-stage-because-of-all-the -spitting-lora-logic-on-punk-prayer-and-poly-styrene.
6. Logic, interview with the author.
7. Ibid.
8. For more on this, see John A. Walker, *Cross-Overs: Art into Pop / Pop into Art* (London: Routledge, 1987), 79–85.
9. Logic, quoted in Cook, "The Essentially Perilous Logic of Lora," 17.
10. Logic, interview with the author.
11. Ibid.
12. Ibid.
13. Logic, quoted in Cook, "The Essentially Perilous Logic of Lora," 17.

14. Logic, interview with the author.
15. Ibid.
16. Don Cherry, quoted in Vivien Goldman, "Don Cherry: Black Gypsy, Folk Dreams," *Melody Maker* (September 22, 1979).
17. Logic, interview with the author.
18. See Simon Reynolds, *Rip It Up and Start Again: Post-Punk, 1978–1984* (London: Faber and Faber, 2005).

8

A Tribe Called Quest, "Can I Kick It?" (1990)

Generations

At the cusp of the 1990s, A Tribe Called Quest utilize a bass sample from a rock song as a vehicle to fuse jazz and hip-hop. Underpinned by the collaboration of the band's members—rapper and producer Q-Tip, DJ Ali Shaheed Muhammad, and rappers Phife Dawg and Jarobi White—"Can I Kick It?" inventively fuses generations by entering into a dialogue with the musician Herbie Flowers, who made the original sample.[1] Structured as a call-and-response song, its title phrase underlines the protagonist's desire to collaborate with other musicians. When Q-Tip asks, "Can I kick it?," the collective response from the rest of the band is "Yes, you can!" The key to the fusion of generations and genres on the track is the way it collapses time by emphasizing sonic space. Here, fusion permits A Tribe Called Quest to retool elements of the past into an expressive vehicle in the present.

"Can I Kick It?" opens with Flowers's bass riff from Lou Reed's "Walk on the Wild Side" (produced by David Bowie in 1972).[2] Drawing on the bassist's extensive experience in jazz bands in the previous decade, of all the samples they've utilized throughout their work—including Weather Report's fusion of jazz and rock on "Young and Fine" on their track "Butter" (1991)—Flowers's is arguably the most dynamic due to its unique spatial qualities.

Since A Tribe Called Quest were always keen for their engineer Bob Power to enhance the presence of the bass within their sound, it's no coincidence that a sample from a bass-heavy track is chosen to underpin "Can I Kick It?" "We asked him, 'How do we get it to become fatter?'" Ali recalls, and "he replied, 'Well, you guys can just put some tones underneath the bass.'"[3] This is precisely what the band do by sampling Flowers's riff, with its electric bass subtly pulsing beneath the acoustic double bass. On their next LP, *The Low End Theory* (1991), the band extend this fascination by working with bassist Ron Carter (alumni of Miles Davis's quartet in the 1960s and bass anchor for CTI Records in the 1970s).

Following the bass, the other key sample used on the track—the proto-boom-bap beat from funk-driven jazz organist Lonnie Smith's "Spinning Wheel" (1970), played by drummer Joe Dukes—starts up and "Can I Kick It?" surges forward. "When I chose which samples to use, there wasn't a perfect equation to it. For me, it was about what sounded dope," Q-Tip remembers.[4] The way the two samples are utilized as a sonic bed for Q-Tip and Phife to rhyme over is precisely that. Carefully sequenced together, the swing in the bass riff and the stuttering drumbeat build a rhythmic complexity into the track, the push and pull between the two cultivating a torqued sense of space. Jarobi describes hip-hop in the late 1980s as consisting mostly of "straight 4/4, 808 drums, and James Brown samples, everything on the one," and it not being "until [A Tribe Called Quest], and a couple of other groups [...] that [hip-hop] started getting movement."[5] This sense of movement is central to the spatial dynamic established by "Can I Kick It?"

Q-Tip's sampling sensibility is honed by making so-called pause tapes in his early teens while growing up in Queens, New York. Using dual cassette decks, he assembled beats by recording a sample of a break beat—the part of a track featuring just the drummer—from another tape. Pausing it when the sample finished a rotation, Q-Tip then rewound to the beginning of the sample and unpaused the tape, repeating the process until there's a loop lasting several minutes. This rude but inventive method was born from necessity. "We didn't have any track machines. What we usually had was some janky-ass stereo system that your moms and your grandmother had."[6] Armed with these tapes, Q-Tip began to put what became the band's first LP together: "I did a lot of *People's Instinctive Travels* [...] already on pause-tapes [...] when I was in the tenth grade at sixteen years old."[7] Ali's early experience with making tapes was similar. Q-Tip saw him perform and asked him to make a mixtape. "So I made the tape and I don't remember what I put in there but I had mad records. He liked it and that's how [...] we formed the group."[8]

With the bass-and-drum pattern established, the vocals for "Can I Kick It?" come next. Q-Tip's voice enters with the title phrase, lagging behind the beat a little more each time it's repeated. "One thing Tip didn't need was coaching," says Ali about his band member's rapping, "he had a real understanding of timing, cadence, and flows."[9] Debuted on the Jungle Brothers's "Black Is Black" in 1988 and then developed on De La Soul's "Buddy" a year later, Q-Tip's voice acquires its distinctive bubble-gum timbre by the time "Can I Kick It?" came out in 1990. After Q-Tip is repeatedly invited to join in by the rest of the band in the track's opening line, the first verse starts with the invitation being extended to the listener, with Q-Tip rapping, "To all the people who can Quest like A Tribe does / Before this, did you really know what live was?" Besides bringing the listener into the song, by addressing them directly the line also serves to recap the origins of the band's name (first referred to by Q-Tip as "A Tribe" on the demo to the Jungle Brothers track "Promo" in 1988 and lengthening to "A Tribe Called Quest" in the lyrics for the released version of the song later in the year). The newly minted name gives a sense of not only the band's collective nature but also it being premised on a process of perpetual searching—a quality essential to fusion.

The distinctive character of Q-Tip's voice is highlighted when an earnest-sounding Phife takes the second verse, coming down squarely on the beat each time the title phrase is repeated. Besides a different feel for timing, their approach to lyrics (Phife begins to pen them only a year later for *Low End Theory*) is crucial to the band's collaborative dynamic. "The combo always worked really well," claims Q-Tip of their vocal contrast.[10] "Phife was always the battle rapper—he would take what was happenin' on the street and rhyme about it [...] and he was a great freestyler as well. My shit was always more cerebral."[11] Phife's rapping on the track highlights less Phife "the battle rapper" and more the distinctive timbre and timing of Q-Tip's own voice.

A self-taught musicologist, Q-Tip sees that the link between jazz and hip-hop ran further back than even the fusion of rock and jazz in the late 1960s—the starting point for most historians and critics—all the way to bebop in the 1940s (as it did for contemporaries Freestyle Fellowship). Referring to himself with the moniker "the Abstract," against the bass sample on "Excursions" from *The Low End Theory*, Q-Tip rhymes "You could find the Abstract listening to hip-hop / My pops used to say, it reminded him of bebop." The tendency of both hip-hop and bebop to cut up traditional structures of popular music using staccato rhythms is analyzed through familial memories. Expanding on this in an interview, Q-Tip insists on how "that line [...] is true [...] based on the improvisation of jazz and [...] the free styling of hip-hop."[12] With jazz, "if somebody is playing a solo and improvising, they are searching for something melodically," and likewise with hip-hop, rappers "are searching for something lyrically."[13] Asked to define A Tribe Called Quest in terms of the genres the band fused, Q-Tip replies: "We shoot ourselves in the foot when we start leaning on the crutch of a category. [...] Let's just call it music."[14] Ali was similarly cautious:

"Now every rap record coming out has some type of jazz groove to it [...] and that might be a problem."[15] (Ali is perhaps thinking of the way acid jazz—in the guise of Guru's Jazzmatazz project and the band Us3 from the early 1990s—pursued an avenue that turned out to be a dead-end as it emphasizes fusion as style rather than process.)

For Q-Tip, the crucial historical figure in fusion is Miles Davis, who similarly rejects the use of labels such as "jazz fusion" (and even "jazz"). Davis starts out by accompanying one of the pioneers of bebop, Charlie Parker, before first piloting cool jazz in the late 1940s, modal jazz in the late 1950s, and hard-bop in the mid-1960s. While these developments rely on acoustic instruments, Davis's LPs from 1968 onward that fuse jazz with rock and feature electric instruments are essential to Q-Tip: "When Miles was doing *Sorcerer* [1967] and all of a sudden [...] did *Bitches Brew* [1970]," with its electric guitar and keyboard, it "flipped his whole sound."[16] As a result of the shift to electric instruments, Davis's use of space became more pronounced. Discussing the LP *People's Instinctive Travels and the Paths of Rhythm* (featuring "Can I Kick It?"), Q-Tip remarks: "Around the time I was making that album I was reading a Miles Davis interview and he was talking about the musicality of space and how space is used [... and] I was like 'man, it's what is between the notes that makes it stick out.'"[17] Q-Tip applies this to each of the tracks on the debut LP. "When I first did 'Bonita [Applebum]' it was a straight rhyme and then I came back to it maybe like a few months later and broke it down like a conversation. I just started thinking about space, you know what I mean? It was there within me, but then the Miles [interview], after hearing what he said [...] it became

more defined, like 'Aha,' you know what I mean?"[18]
Q-Tip uses the same process on "Can I Kick It?"

The sense of space Q-Tip is drawn to in Davis's music is courtesy of his producer Teo Macero. Macero carefully constructs Davis's LPs in the late 1960s and early 1970s from hours of session reels. As if to highlight this, on the track "Yesternow" from 1971's *Jack Johnson*, Macero uses a sample from Davis's *In a Silent Way*, recorded two years earlier, dropping in a brief segment midway through the track (and again at its very end). Introducing a unique sense of sonic and temporal space into a track with the interloping of two different sources and their respective moments of recording, Macero's editing is an early example of sampling. This prefigures many of the techniques that would become common practice in hip-hop decades later.

By isolating the bass riff from "Walk on the Wild Side," with its distinctive pause between each run of notes, Q-Tip channels the spatial architecture of the track. Engineer Bob Power is highly attuned to the spatiotemporal complexity taking place on "Can I Kick It?" This was "really one of the first times [...] where very intricate musical constructions were made from samples," Power notes.[19] "It sounded like everybody meant to play that stuff together because it was on this new [...] polygroove. At the same time, it could never possibly have been played by people sitting down in a traditional sense," as both the samples and the vocals were recorded in different places across various time periods.[20] A Tribe Called Quest's producer is crucial to the careful coordination of these disparate spatial and temporal elements. "When we brought music samples in, Bob made sure things were tuned a certain way," says Ali, since "sometimes, when we

87

were collecting samples, all of them weren't in the same key."[21] As their samplers—the SP-1200 and Akai S950—don't have a lot of memory, the band find themselves "taking a record and speeding it up and putting it on a 45—like a regular 33 LP," explains Ali, "to be sure it could get into the sampler, but then we had to pitch it down with these little different things and tricks" to synchronize them.[22] Following Q-Tip and Ali's selection, Power's engineering makes the asynchronous sound synchronous, with space feeling continuous rather than carefully constructed.

Where Macero the producer and Davis the musician—or indeed Bowie the producer and Flowers the musician—are two distinct people, Q-Tip absorbs both these roles in A Tribe Called Quest, channeling Macero's spatial sensibility by way of the sampled bass riff. The recording studio is essential to the producer and artist becoming one. Referring to himself as "a studio rat," Q-Tip describes how "those tools in the studio became extensions of my imagination and thoughts."[23] Besides the collaboration between different members of the band, the studio is also the site of collaboration for the Native Tongues collective, which also includes De La Soul, Jungle Brothers, Monie Love, and Queen Latifah. "In the studio, we had the [Native Tongues] there around us," says Jarobi, providing "a great sense of camaraderie."[24] Depicting groups of people rendered in silhouette, Paije Hunyady and Bryant Peters's cover for *People's Instinctive Travels and the Paths of Rhythm* conveys the sense of the collective nature of the group.

Balanced against this collaborative approach is the dominant role Q-Tip assumes in A Tribe Called Quest, with Jarobi attesting to how "Q-Tip was definitely the leader of the group."[25] Later, Q-Tip reveals how the use of the Tribe moniker for the purposes of production was spurious. "I never put on [...] 'produced by Q-Tip' [...] because it wasn't about that [...] it was about the Tribe, so I put 'produced by A Tribe Called Quest.'"[26] Eventually, Q-Tip's dominant role—as he perpetually cultivates fusion—causes tension, leading to the demise of the group.

Collapsing time by emphasizing space, the fusion taking place on "Can I Kick It?" acts as a vehicle for A Tribe Called Quest to foreground their emotional intelligence in a genre later criticized for its misogyny. In time, this triggers a younger generation of musicians' pursuit of the fusion of jazz and hip-hop, from the Roots' *Do You Want More?!!!??!* (1995), all the way through to Kendrick Lamar's *To Pimp a Butterfly* (2015) and Moor Mother's *Jazz Codes* (2022).

1. See Justin A. Williams "The Construction of Jazz Rap as High Art in Hip-Hop Music," *Journal of Musicology* 27, no. 4 (Fall 2010): 435–59; and James McNally, "A Love Interrupted: A Tribe Called Quest's Resilient Path of Rhythm," *Global Hip Hop Studies 1*, no. 1 (June 2020): 175–97.

2. See Michael Schloss, *Making Beats: The Art of Sample-Based Hip Hop* (Middletown, CT: Wesleyan University Press, 2004).

3. Ali Shaheed Muhammad, quoted in Chris Williams, "Footprints," *Wax Poetics*, no. 65, 2017, 64.

4. Q-Tip, quoted in ibid., 65.

5. Jarobi White, quoted in Harry Allen, liner notes, A Tribe Called Quest, *People's Instinctive Travels and the Paths of Rhythm*, 25th Anniversary Edition (Columbia Records, 2015).

6. Q-Tip (lecture, Red Bull Music Academy, New York, 2013), www. redbullmusicacademy.com/lectures/q-tip.

7. Q-Tip, quoted in Keith Murphy, "Full Clip: Q-Tip Runs Down His Music Catalogue," *VIBE* (July 15, 2011), https://www.vibe.com/gallery/full -clip-q-tip-runs-down-his-music-catalogue-ft-tribe-de-la-soul-nas -biggie-roots/promo-jungle-brothers-q-tip/.

8. Ali Shaheed Muhammad (lecture, Red Bull Music Academy, Los Angeles, 2012), https://www.redbullmusicacademy.com/lectures /ali-shaheed-muhammad-2012.

9. Ali, quoted in Williams, "Footprints," 59.

10. Q-Tip, quoted in "A Tribe Called Quest," *The Anthology of Rap*, ed. Adam Bradley and Andrew DuBois (New Haven, CT: Yale University Press, 2010), 305.

11. Ibid.

12. Q-Tip, quoted in *Beats, Rhymes & Life: The Travels of a Tribe Called Quest*, directed by Michael Rapaport (Los Angeles: Sony Picture Classics, 2011).

13. Ibid.

14. Q-Tip, quoted in Miles Marshall Lewis, "Abstract Poetics," *The Source* (April 2002).

15. Ali, quoted in Janine McAdams and Havelock Nelson, "The New Jazz Swing Takes Shape: Artists Are Fusing Styles into a New Form," *Billboard* (August 29, 1992): 21.

16. Q-Tip, quoted in Miles Marshall Lewis, "After the Love Is Gone: A Tribe Called Quest," *The Source* (October 1998).

17. Q-Tip (lecture, Red Bull Music Academy).

18. Ibid.

19. Bob Power, quoted in Shawn Taylor, "Twenty Questions with Bob Power," in *People's Instinctive Travels and the Paths of Rhythm* (London: Bloomsbury, 2007), 109.

20. Ibid., 110.

21. Ali, quoted in Williams, "Footprints," 67.

22. Ibid., 67.

23. Q-Tip, quoted in ibid.

24. Jarobi, quoted in ibid.

25. Ibid.

26. Q-Tip (lecture, Red Bull Music Academy).

9

Kendrick Lamar and Kamasi Washington, "u" (2015)

Histories

No track before or after Kendrick Lamar's "u" fuses jazz with hip-hop so forcefully. Driving Lamar's fusion of genres is a compelling fusion of histories: the coarse lyrics and vocal force of hip-hop from the late 1980s is channeled by Lamar's rapping and the mindfulness of the progressive jazz movement of the 1970s is fed through Washington's tenor saxophone. Arguably embracing more complex forms of instrumentation than previously attempted in hip-hop, "u" is a type of conscious rap steeped in jazz instrumentation that juxtaposes sonic extremes. Lamar uses this fusion of genres and histories as an expressive vehicle to deal with the consequences of the critical and commercial success of his second LP, *good kid, m.A.A.d city* (2012).

As "u" opens, the tinkling of a piano is followed by the echo of a loud scream. Disturbingly, the scream bounces around, conveying the intensity of the feelings the song is premised on. "u" storyboards the anxiety Lamar feels while looking at himself in a hotel mirror during a tour, after learning that a friend's younger brother has been murdered. "I was able to bottle that moment and put it on record," Lamar says.[1] As "u" begins, Washington's full-throated tenor saxophone takes center stage and Lamar continues to scream until a bass-heavy rhythm emerges out of the sonic soup. "Loving you is complicated!" shouts Lamar as a gruff flurry of notes comes from the saxophone. Contrasting with the rasp of the horn and the growl of the vocal, the tinkling piano in the background provides a momentary sense of delicacy. Both the saxophone and the piano soon fall away, and the first verse opens with Lamar spitting out lyrics, rapid-fire, in step with the pace and attack of the saxophone. "Feel like you ain't shit, feel like you don't feel," and later in the verse, "Fuckin' hate you, I hope you embrace it, I swear." The degree of self-hatred becomes more acute as the verses unfold, making for difficult listening.

The fusion of jazz and hip-hop on "u" is undergirded by two moments in the history of these genres, which are specific to where Lamar grew up in South Central Los Angeles. The first reaches Lamar directly and involves late 1980s hip-hop group N.W.A., particularly Dr. Dre, who Lamar saw on the street as a child: "I was about eight years old, they was shooting a video in my neighborhood in Compton [and] my father [...] put me on his shoulders and there they was."[2] Decades later, the sighting remained vivid in Lamar's mind, the same street serving as the location for the video of "King Kunta," a single on *To Pimp a Butterfly* (2015). As a collaborator and mentor, Dre plays an important role in Lamar's music, serving as executive producer of both *good kid, m.A.A.d city* (including contributing vocally to the track "Compton") and, three years later, *To Pimp a Butterfly*. If the deep bottom end Dre carves out in the late 1980s with N.W.A. (courtesy of Parliament samples) is crucial to Lamar, then lyrically it's Ice Cube's politically barbed verses on N.W.A.'s tracks like the band's 1988 "Straight Outta Compton."

The second moment in South Central LA history, which is less well-known and reached Lamar indirectly through Washington, involves the jazz musician and Locke High School teacher Reggie Andrews, who mentored Washington (as well as other jazz musicians playing on *To Pimp a Butterfly*, including bassist Thundercat, trumpeter Ryan Porter, and producer Terrace Martin).[3] The leader of Reggie Andrews and the Fellowship in the 1960s and keyboardist for the funk-laced jazz group Karma in the 1970s, Andrews later became dedicated to teaching a new generation of musicians. As a result, by the time these musicians collaborate with Lamar, each is steeped in a type of jazz cut with funk and electronica. Fusion helps the younger generation turn around general perceptions of jazz, eschewing the "America's classical music" tag it was lumped with courtesy of Wynton Marsalis, in favor of something both more contemporary and inclusive. Washington comments: "[Jazz] has been trapped in this image of something that is a historic relic, or something that is made to serve some purpose other than to just enjoy. And I think it's a music that, it's the reverse. It's such an expressive music, and when you hear jazz, you really hear a commune of people who are expressing themselves together."[4] Washington's approach to jazz makes the saxophonist the perfect collaborator for Lamar.

Lamar is acutely aware of the way his sensibility has been formed through these two historical strands: "I was raised in an environment where [...] my father was a complete realist in the streets and my mother [...] a dreamer, [so] it starts there [...] before I ever heard any type of melody or lyric. That's the DNA of who I am today; the yin and the yang."[5] Rather than being turned into a harmonious blend, Lamar fuses elements of hip-hop and jazz in such a way as to maintain a sense of tension.

Collaboration with musicians grounded in either hip-hop or jazz plugs Lamar into different notions of community. Partly, this comes by way of the collaboration with the LA jazz community, represented by Washington, but Lamar also approaches the notion of community as a concept in itself. "These were my experiences [...] this is my life that I'm talking 'bout. I'm not speaking to the community. I'm not speaking of the community. I am the community."[6] By no coincidence, the community responds in kind. "The album means so much, not only to Compton, but to Los Angeles as a whole," stresses Lalah Hathaway, a vocalist on *To Pimp a Butterfly* (and daughter of soul singer Donny Hathaway).[7] "Speaking as a person who lives in this community," Hathaway continues, "it means so much for [Kendrick] to reach back and give these kids their dreams in the palms of their hands."[8] Besides spotlighting the cultural importance of hip-hop by winning Grammy awards for *To Pimp a Butterfly* and even a Pulitzer Prize for his next LP, Lamar also develops after-school programs for music and sports in the Compton Unified School District. Despite criticizing himself of the obverse throughout each consecutive verse of "u," Lamar's sense of community is acute.

After the first verse, "u" slips into a drawn-out middle section. A chorus of voices sing, and a drumbeat is panned from left to right, before a Hispanic voice cuts through, exclaiming "Housekeeping, housekeeping!" As they compete, the different vocal timbres create a scene in which Lamar is dealing with a near-schizophrenic moment before the hotel mirror.

Unsurprisingly, given the complex fusion of jazz and hip-hop on "u," writing and recording the track involves Lamar stretching himself considerably. The subject matter of the song shaped the mood of the session, which "was very uncomfortable," recalls the mixing engineer MixedByAli: "the mic was on and I could hear him walking back and forth [...] having these super angry vocals."[9] The lyrics are composed in the booth on the spot. "It was super emotional. I never asked what got into him that day."[10] The degree of discomfort is worth enduring, as it generates one of Lamar's most affecting combinations of lyrics and vocal tone.

Featuring Lamar spitting the lines in the same rapid-fire way as earlier verses but with an increased sense of desperation, the tone becomes alarmingly distraught as "u" moves into its second verse.

By its middle, Lamar discloses his guilt following the death of his friend's younger brother.[11] "A friend never leave Compton for profit, or leave his best friend, little brother / You promised you'd watch him before they shot him." As the lyrics detail the precise events, guilt edges into self-loathing. "When I was on that tour bus," explains Lamar, "things is happening back home in my city or in my family that I can't do nothing about."[12] Survivor's guilt, and the distance wedged between him and his community through wealth and fame, runs through Lamar's reflections on the events. "It's real, man […] three of my homeboys […] was murdered" — "I gotta get back off that tour bus and go to these funerals, talk to their mas and aunties."[13]

More lyrical and less raspy than before, in between the second and third verses, Washington's saxophone playing continues. On the third verse Lamar provides an analysis of the situation conveyed earlier, opening with the line "I know your secrets, nigga, mood swings is frequent, nigga / I know depression is restin' on your heart for two reasons, nigga." Lamar's voice becomes increasingly distraught, peaking with the last couplet: "You should've felt that black revolver blast a long time ago / And if these mirrors could talk it'd say, 'You gotta go.'" The track concludes with the line "And if I told your secrets the world'll know money can't stop a suicidal weakness." Lamar later reflected: "[These events] can draw a thin line between you having your sanity and you losing it, […] psychologically, it messes your brain up."[14] The survivor's guilt triggers a sense of deep anxiety. "It was real uncomfortable," says Lamar of the period, "because I was dealing with my own issues. I was making a transition from the lifestyle that I lived before to the one I have now. When you're onstage rapping and all these people are cheering for you, you actually feel like you're saving lives. But you aren't saving lives back home. It made me question if I am in the right place."[15] The result of the anxiety is depression. "That was one of the hardest songs I had to write. [...] There's some very dark moments in there. All my insecurities and selfishness and let downs. That shit is depressing as a motherfucker."[16]

The beats and vocals for "u" were already laid down when Martin, the producer, decided to call on other members of South Central LA's jazz community to add live instrumentation. Besides an existing relationship with Martin, Washington was also then a key figure among the younger generation of LA-based jazz musicians. The tenor saxophone on "u" contributes not only to the sonic color of the backing but at times jumps out and acts like an alternative voice to Lamar's. Washington's collaboration with Lamar comes after the recording of his debut LP, a sprawling triple-disc affair aptly titled *The Epic* (2015). The same intensity of *To Pimp a Butterfly* is embedded in the grooves of *The Epic*. "When Terrace heard the strings and choir [on *The Epic*] his eyes lit up [...] and he said 'man, I've got something you should work on with Kendrick.'"[17] A date is made to meet with Lamar at the recording studio. "They showed me the original song they wanted me to do [and] to give me the full scope of what that [...] meant they played me the whole album."[18] Successive listening sessions follow. "Every time they played the album [...] they found a new song they wanted me to write something for."[19] Washington's playing and arranging pepper the LP, but nowhere is his tenor saxophone more noticeable than on "u."

Besides Washington and Thundercat, keyboardist Robert Glasper and trombonist Ryan Porter are also invited to participate late in the recording process. "Once it got to the point where it was almost done and sounding good, that's when Kendrick started coming in like, 'I wanna hear how this track came out. Because I know it was hot before I left and I want to hear what these people did.'"[20] The additional element Lamar is searching for was provided by the jazz musicians. Porter continues: "He'd come in later and the energy would change. These instruments started giving these tracks a different spirit, a different energy. [...] He started coming in and checking out the vibe of these songs, like, 'Oh, he's got Thundercat on this one!' All these different things were adding all these different colors."[21] Knowing "u" would have sounded very different without Washington and the other musicians, Lamar and Martin are careful about the way jazz is used. "They didn't use jazz samples, and they didn't need old jazz musicians," Glasper says of the *To Pimp a Butterfly* sessions.[22] "That's the 'real hip-hop meets jazz' right there. That was something I was already doing in my world, but for Kendrick to do it, it changed everything."[23] Three years earlier, Glasper's *Black Radio* (2012) fused jazz with hip-hop, but Lamar's *To Pimp a Butterfly* does so with more impact due to his popularity.

Lamar explains how the title *To Pimp a Butterfly* is itself a fusion of extremes: "I just really wanted to show the brightness of life and the word 'pimp' has so much aggression."[24] The music's sonic and lyrical fusion is further played out in Denis Rouvre's photo collage on the LP's cover, depicting black men in vests brandishing fistfuls of banknotes superimposed in front of the White House. The way the two extremes are spliced together serves to drive Lamar's point home. Typified by "u," the entire sonic and visual package of *To Pimp a Butterfly* gains its dynamism from being premised on a fusion of genres, sensibilities, and communities, providing Lamar with the tools to express acute feelings of guilt at a key moment in his personal and creative development.

1. Kendrick Lamar, quoted in Marcus J. Moore, *The Butterfly Affect: How Kendrick Lamar Ignited the Soul of Black America* (London: Hodder & Stoughton, 2020), 20.
2. Kendrick Lamar, "Seeing Dr. Dre and Tupac as a Kid," Recording Academy, October 8, 2013, https://www.youtube.com/watch?v=KdUhlV_Si2E.
3. See Steven Isoardi, *The Dark Tree: Jazz and the Community Arts in Los Angeles* (Berkeley, CA: University of California Press, 2006).
4. Kamasi Washington, quoted in Nate Chinen, "Change of the Guard," *Playing Changes: Jazz for the New Century* (New York: Pantheon Books, 2018), 4.
5. Kendrick Lamar, "Kendrick Lamar Meets Rick Rubin and They Have an Epic Conversation," interview by Rick Rubin, *GQ* (October 20, 2016), https://www.youtube.com/watch?v=4lPD5PtqMiE.
6. Lamar, quoted in Moore, *The Butterfly Affect*, 157.
7. Lelah Hathaway, quoted in ibid., 173.
8. Ibid.
9. MixedByAli, quoted in Andreas Hale, "The Oral History of Kendrick Lamar's *To Pimp a Butterfly*," *Medium* (February 9, 2016), https://medium.com/cuepoint/the-oral-history-of-kendrick-lamar-s-to-pimp-a-butterfly-622f725c3fde.
10. Ibid.
11. See "Articulations of Displacement and Dissonance from Compton: Kendrick Lamar in the Twenty-First Century," *Global Hip Hop Studies* 2, no. 1 (June 2021): 93–114.
12. Kendrick Lamar, "Kendrick Lamar Talks about 'u,' His Depression & Suicidal Thoughts (Pt. 2)," MTV News, April 1, 2015, https://www.youtube.com/watch?v=Hu4Pz9PjolI.
13. Ibid.
14. Ibid.
15. Lamar, quoted in Hale, "Oral History."
16. Lamar, quoted in "*To Pimp a Butterfly*: A Track-By-Track Guide," *Rolling Stone* (Australia) (March 17, 2015), https://au.rollingstone.com/music/music-news/kendrick-lamars-to-pimp-a-butterfly-a-track-by-track-guide-609/.
17. Kamasi Washington, "Interview about *The Epic*," AOL Build, December 28, 2017, https://www.youtube.com/watch?v=JvTqmNOpzZU.

18. Ibid.
19. Ibid.
20. Ryan Porter, quoted in Moore, *The Butterfly Affect*, 171.
21. Ibid., 171–172.
22. Robert Glasper, quoted in ibid., 168.
23. Ibid.
24. Kendrick Lamar, quoted in Colin Stutz, "Kendrick Lamar's Latest Album Wasn't Always Called 'To Pimp a Butterfly,'" *Billboard*, March 31, 2015, https://www.billboard.com/music/rb-hip-hop/kendrick-lamar-to-pimp-a-butterfly-caterpillar-album-title-6517089/.

10

Neneh Cherry and Four Tet,
"Natural Skin Deep" (2018)

Eras

Asked in an interview, "Was it just normal for
you to fuse different styles?" Neneh Cherry replies:
"Something that I've taken with me from my
upbringing, was a kind of borderless philosophy.
It was more about making your own sound and
taking these influences and ideas in a fearless way."[1]
Cherry puts this into practice by fusing free jazz,

hip-hop, and electronic music—as well as the four distinct eras of her development—on "Natural Skin Deep." Starting out by layering jazz and post-punk in the band Rip Rig + Panic in 1981, from the late 1980s to the late 1990s Cherry explores hip-hop and pop, then in the aughts blends electronic music and rap, and in 2012 she returns to jazz and post-punk. "Natural Skin Deep"—from Cherry's 2018's *Broken Politics*—fuses all three genres (jazz, hip-hop, and electronic music) by staging her four-decade personal journey through music.

Considering the richness of Cherry's relationship to jazz—her stepfather is the free-jazz trumpeter Don Cherry—and her "borderless philosophy," it's appropriate that the sonic key of "Natural Skin Deep" is translation. "We're influenced by everything that's happening around us," Cherry reasons, "but [the key is] to then translate it through your own signals."[2] While Cherry has constantly translated one genre into the terms of another, "Natural Skin Deep" feels like a late-period high in a career propelled by fusion. Collaboration with a range of producers from the 1980s to the present is crucial to this. Cherry's most dynamic fusion of jazz comes not directly by working with musicians from within the genre, but indirectly through her collaboration with a single musician outside of it, Kieran Hebden (a.k.a. Four Tet). Hebden's production of "Natural Skin Deep" references Cherry's past by incorporating a sample of a track featuring free-jazz saxophonist Ornette Coleman playing with her stepfather.

Cherry begins making music professionally in the early 1980s with the band Rip Rig + Panic (named after the 1965 jazz LP by the Roland Kirk Quartet). Coleman and Don Cherry's recordings from the 1960s are crucial to the band. Their "sonic experimentation didn't just divide opinion," Cherry recalls in her obit for Coleman, "it incensed some people. It was hardcore. It was like punk in a way—total confrontation."[3] If free jazz informed Rip Rig + Panic's approach on their three LPs, Don Cherry's playing on their second LP, *I Am Cold* (1982), ensured its fervor made it onto the record.[4]

Positioned midway through "Natural Skin Deep," after the sound of a rave siren, the free-jazz sample Hebden uses is lifted from Coleman's "Growing Up," recorded in 1969. Featuring the piercing squeak of his saxophone alongside Don Cherry's trumpet, the sample is like a pause on the track, as if the producer is waiting for the listener's memory to catch on by recalling Cherry's past before continuing. A second siren goes off and the main body of the song continues.

Fusing hip-hop and pop, Cherry's second era starts in 1986 with an early version of "Buffalo Stance." "To a certain extent, it's where I come from, but I'm not a straight rapper. Going both ways has just come naturally."[5] Titled "Looking Good Diving" and produced by the Wild Bunch, the track appeared on the B-side to a single by pop duo Morgan McVey. Rerecorded two years later by Cherry and released as her debut solo single, the Tim Simenon-produced "Buffalo Stance" became a global hit. Cherry sung each chorus of "Buffalo Stance" while rapping the verses, a pattern largely continued throughout the rest of the LP, *Raw Like Sushi*, with McVey joining the production team. Cherry and McVey married in 1990, and her next two solo LPs, 1992's *Homebrew* and 1996's *Man*, featured her continually moving between the two forms of vocal delivery.

During the fade-out of "Natural Skin Deep" Cherry edges into rapping.[6] As she repeatedly sings the hook from the chorus ("My love goes on and on"), her double-tracked voice interjects with the rap, "Here's one for the great Sioux nation / Bla bla for a generation." The second time the chorus is repeated in the fade-out, Cherry raps, "No living on station / Pumping that black gold over the hill / Recycle evolution while killing free will." The movement between the two forms of vocal delivery is key to the track. "Singing and melody can take you to all kinds of places and then the rap brings you down to earth."[7] The commentary on contemporary social politics— as the Standing Rock tribe of Sioux fought to halt the Dakota Access Pipeline in 2016—provided by the rap complements the politics of the self the song's sung lyrics explore.

Cherry's third era involves the fusion of electronic music and hip-hop, beginning with tracks from 1989's *Raw Like Sushi*, featuring Robert Del Naja and Andrew Vowles, who were transitioning from the loose collective the Wild Bunch into the group Massive Attack. Their remix of Cherry's "Manchild" in 1989 is part of the opening salvo of trip-hop, the genre fusing electronic music with hip-hop. Demoed in her London flat, and coproduced by McVey, "Hymn of the Big Wheel," from the band's debut LP *Blue Lines* (1991), is partly composed by Cherry.

On both sides of the sample on "Natural Skin Deep," and prior to the concluding rap, a loping electronic beat with a bass pulsing underneath propels the track forward. Hebden sweetens the track considerably by using synthesized swooshes that zip from one side of the sound stage to another. Except for the middle section, Cherry's voice is central throughout.

Known for capturing the techno club scene of the 1980s and 1990s, Wolfgang Tillmans is commissioned to take the photograph used for the LP cover, which depicts Cherry standing grounded in the middle of a blustery London street.

Returning full circle, in the early aughts, Cherry fuses jazz with post-punk, in collaboration with the jazz group the Thing (named after a Don Cherry track). "That record was such an important record [...] because I remembered who I was," and "working in such an experimental way was such a big part of my heritage that I hadn't really tapped into since Rip Rig + Panic days."[8] *The Cherry Thing* (2012), recorded in just a handful of sessions, pits songs written by Coleman and Don Cherry with those by proto-punk group Suicide and the rapper MF Doom. *The Cherry Thing* remix LP (2012) is Cherry's first collaboration with Hebden; it's an album that stretches the dynamic range of the original by adding and subtracting instrumentation. With an intro highlighting the subtle vibraphone playing on the original, Hebden's remix of "Dream Baby Dream" inserts an electronic beat, heightening the fusion between jazz, hip-hop, and electronic music while emphasizing the distinct timbre of Cherry's voice.

Cherry and McVey are drawn to Hebden's output as Four Tet, in which the musician and producer "discover[ed] that I was into electronic music, and that I had finally found a medium where I felt I was able to really do something that broke down some boundaries."[9] Prior to collaborating with Cherry, Hebden reconfigured house, dubstep, and ambient music on a compelling sequence of solo LPs. "Once I started making music on computer, I found that there were all sorts of possibilities."[10] Between 2006 and 2008, Hebden collaborated on four LPs with the jazz drummer Steve Reid, with the aim to create "a twist on contemporary electronic music, to see that music [...] brought into this improvisational context."[11] Cherry's initial invitation to Hebden in 2012 makes sense given her collaborations with both electronic and jazz musicians. Following the remix of "Dream Baby Dream," Hebden's first production of a new track by Cherry is a duet with Afrika Baby Bam of the Jungle Brothers in 2013. Hebden then produces the entirety of *Blank Project* in 2014, and four years later, *Broken Politics*. Cherry and Hebden's dynamic collaboration is key to *Broken Politics*. "The reason I value the relationship so much with Kieran is his insight sonically feels so spot-on. I feel like he can see the things I'm feeling and bring them out."[12] "That's what's so beautiful about the magic of collaboration," Cherry continues, "I bring my bits and Kieran does his thing, but you're kind of gently pushing each other with these ideas."[13]

The recording process behind "Natural Skin Deep" involves a fusion of two different approaches to the studio. Recorded live, Cherry's vocals for *Broken Politics* are cut partly in the Creative Music Studio in Woodstock, New York (cofounded by Coleman in the early 1970s and frequented by her stepfather). Despite this analog setup, "I made the whole thing in the computer," Hebden says. "I knew I was making something that was going to evoke the mood, that you would listen to it and it would sound like there were a group of musicians playing there. But nothing like that happened at all, ever."[14] Due to her personal history with the space, Cherry insists on how "the music is made for real, even if it's loops and is coming from a computer. [...] To me there are definitely sounds and a feeling in some of the tracks that remind me of the music that was made in the room, some of the music that brought me to where I'm sitting at now."[15] Hebden's use of the sample in the middle of "Natural Skin Deep" is central to this fusion of recording processes. While the sample captures Coleman and Don Cherry playing their acoustic instruments in a specific time and space, its reuse is only possible with recourse to technology. The electronic rave siren and the squeal of the saxophone derive from very different places and yet, because of their careful sequencing, seem to mirror each other.

Before even entering the studio, Cherry works intensively on the composition. "I always need to also have time where I go inside, alone, to clear my head and be with my thoughts and get stuff out."[16] Before the political rap placed at the very end of "Natural Skin Deep," Cherry's lyrics explore her vulnerability. "It's hard not to draw from the things that are happening, but the songs then have to come back to a personal place."[17] Sounding like a statement of purpose, the first verse opens with the line "Appealing I'm revealing just some bare / Essentials of me as me." The verse's final line, "Cause I have an allergy to my realness / Like my own self-worth," gives a sense of Cherry tussling with issues of self-confidence. On "Natural Skin Deep" fusion affords Cherry the opportunity to push herself lyrically as well as sonically, commenting on the multiple phases of jazz's fusion with popular music by emphasizing her personal journey through them, a trajectory highlighted by her autobiography *A Thousand Threads: A Memoir* (2024).

1. Neneh Cherry, quoted in Sheryl Garratt, "Neneh Cherry," *Face* (September 1996).
2. Neneh Cherry, quoted in "Neneh Cherry," Qobuz, October 17, 2018, https://www.youtube.com/watch?v=liNEfNN3Nlo&t=93s.
3. Neneh Cherry, "Ornette Coleman Remembered by Neneh Cherry," *Guardian* (December 27, 2015), https://www.theguardian.com /music/2015/dec/27/ornette-coleman-remembered-by-neneh -cherry-jazz-saxophonist.
4. Cherry accompanied her stepfather while he toured in 1979 with the Slits, a band she later joined.
5. Cherry, quoted in Mark Cooper, "Neneh Cherry: Mother Superior," *Q Magazine* (December 1989).
6. On gender and rap, see Tricia Rose, "Bad Sistas: Black Women Rappers and Sexual Politics in Rap Music," *Black Noise: Rap Music and Black Culture in Contemporary America* (Middletown, CT: Wesleyan University Press, 1994), 146–82.
7. Neneh Cherry, quoted in Cooper, "Neneh Cherry."
8. Neneh Cherry, quoted in "Neneh Cherry," *Music Show*, ABC Arts, March 3, 2015, https://www.youtube.com/watch?v =OpCxeVsNX8U&t=5s.
9. Kieren Hebden, interview by Nick Lawrence, *Higher Frequency*, (June 5, 2006), http://higher-frequency.com/e_interview/kieran _hebden/index.htm.
10. Ibid.
11. Ibid.
12. Neneh Cherry, quoted in Rich Juzwiak, "Neneh Cherry's Unending Quest for Freedom," *Jezebel* (October 19, 2018), https://jezebel.com /neneh-cherrys-unending-quest-for-freedom-1829844203.
13. Ibid.
14. Kieren Hebden, quoted in Jon Pareles, "Neneh Cherry Never Stopped Taking Risks," *New York Times* (October 17, 2018), https://www .nytimes.com/2018/10/17/arts/music/neneh-cherry-four-tet-broken -politics.html.
15. Cherry, quoted in ibid.
16. Neneh Cherry, quoted in Khalila Douze, "Catching Up with the Iconic Neneh Cherry," *Fader* (August 30, 2018), https://www.thefader .com/2018/08/30/neneh-cherry-new-album-fourtet-broken-politics -interview.
17. Cherry, quoted in Juzwiak, "Neneh Cherry's Unending Quest."

II

Moor Mother and Wolf Weston, "Evening" (2022)

Communities

With "Evening" Camae Ayewa (a.k.a. Moor Mother) brings together historic communities of jazz musicians with her community in Philadelphia to instigate the fusion of free jazz and hip-hop. The residue accumulated by the time travel lends the track a sound quality Ayewa characterizes as "dusty."[1] Sonically, the softness the dustiness yields could mean the loss of the tension essential to fusion, but Ayewa uses it strategically to draw the listener in.

Ambient swirls of sound act as a backdrop to the two intertwining vocal textures running throughout the brief two minutes and eleven seconds of "Evening." Ayewa's coarse tone on the verses is soothed by the voice of neo-soul vocalist Wolf Weston on the choruses. If the verses project you into the past by stopping off to visit resonant episodes in jazz's history, the chorus perpetually pulls you back to the present with the plea for the future ("I just want to live another day"). The movement back and forth would be too unsettling were it not for the lyrical flow of both vocalists and the way the sound quality of the track's production brings their distinct vocal timbres together.

"Evening" pursues Octavia E. Butler's approach to time travel explored in *Kindred* (1979)—an Afrofuturist novel using time travel to move between the narrator's present in Los Angeles and an early nineteenth-century Maryland plantation where her ancestors are slaves—by refashioning the history of jazz as a reverberating time machine.[2] Mark Dery, who coined the term, defined Afrofuturism as "speculative fiction that treats African-American concerns in the context of twentieth-century technoculture—and, more generally, African-American signification that appropriates images of technology."[3] Afrofuturism is central to Ayewa's fusion of the historic jazz community with her present one in Philadelphia. While technology is explicitly present in the lyrics, it's also registered implicitly both compositionally and sonically via the use of digital sampling—the lo-fi character coming through in its "dusty" quality.[4] The dustiness is further explored in Anthony Molden's mixed-media cover for the album, as if the debris accumulated through time travel has been randomly dropped onto a twelve-inch square surface.

The initial stop "Evening" makes is to Billie Holiday, a vocalist known for fusing jazz with popular music in the form of the protest song. Holiday is "huge [...] for me and maybe I [only] own like two Billie Holiday records," but "her story, what she went through—I think about that every month."[5] "I'm like Billie singing strengths through in the doubt / What the fuck you mean? / We said who sent you pain through like ice cream / Chocolate deluxe, everyone got touched," rhymes Ayewa. The lyrics point to how the pain Holiday endured as an African American performer was sweetened for listeners. Holiday's struggle in a segregated America feeds directly into her 1939 song "Strange Fruit," which details the lynching of African Americans in the South. Despite the gravity of the subject matter, Holiday's voice retains its sweetness on early performances of "Strange Fruit," which Ayewa's lyrics suggest accounts for its accessibility to a broader audience at the time.

The final stop Ayewa makes on "Evening" is at Nina Simone and her legacy. "Spirits in the dark / Let Nina sing, because it don't mean a thing / If it ain't got the blues." Simone includes a version of "Strange Fruit" on 1965's *Pastel Blues*, an LP titled after one of the song's cutting lines ("Pastoral scene of the gallant South / The bulging eyes and the twisted mouth"). Equally biting, Simone's deep voice resounds throughout. "What I was interested in was conveying an emotional message, which meant using everything you've got inside you sometimes to barely make a note," explained Simone, the strain meaning that "sometimes I sound like gravel and sometimes

I sound like coffee and cream."[6] With references to them bookending the song, if it's Holiday's story that resonates most for Ayewa, then it's the deep tone and texture of Simone's voice on "Strange Fruit" informing hers on "Evening."

While Ayewa explores aspects of Holiday's subject matter and Simone's vocal texture, the method of delivery of the verses to "Evening" comes from a more recent vocalist and composer (not name-checked in the song's lyrics): Chuck D of Public Enemy. "A rapper," affirmed Ayewa, "I would say I'm a rapper."[7] Using rap as a tool to highlight systemic racism in US media, experiencing Public Enemy's 1989 tour was liberating for the young Ayewa: "When Terminator X was like, 'Put up your fists' [...] it was all these Black people with their fists up, and my little fist [was up]."[8] Ayewa channels Chuck D's vocal attack across Moor Mother's first three solo studio LPs but dials it down for *Jazz Codes*.

The approach of Public Enemy's production team, the Bomb Squad, to sampling is just as crucial to Ayewa, their manipulation of technology providing her with additional tools to activate jazz's history and fuse it with hip-hop.[9] Like the Bomb Squad (or A Tribe Called Quest), Moor Mother's *Jazz Codes* uses samples of sound lifted from past recordings, but they are so far removed from their source as to be unrecognizable. Ayewa describes these sounds as being "not so much sampled but treated."[10] *Jazz Codes* also features live playing, a form of what Ayewa refers to as "sampling, in real time."[11] Sampling is a fundamental part of the way "Evening" acts as a time machine by literally bringing the past into the present.

Sun Ra Arkestra, from Philadelphia, is particularly pertinent to Ayewa's Afrofuturist time machine (while Sun Ra passed away three decades ago, Ayewa played live with the Arkestra at Carnegie Hall in 2022). "I didn't know anything about Sun Ra," says Ayewa, "[but] that's why when I [arrived in Philadelphia] I was like, 'I'm just gonna be a school kid' and learn."[12] Ayewa quickly came up to speed on the history of jazz in the city. This includes hip-hop groups like Digable Planets and the Roots, who incorporate jazz, but for Ayewa, Sun Ra is the most important figure. "I would organize [events] like [the AfroFuturist Affair]" — a grassroots community platform designed to promote Afrofuturistic concepts by organizing seminars, exhibitions, and concerts—because "the foundation was there. Of Sun Ra playing open in the parks."[13] Besides playing live in public spaces, in the early 1970s members of the Arkestra opened a grocery store called Pharaoh's Den, selling fresh produce alongside their LPs. The store soon became an improvisational classroom for neighborhood residents. Driven by the fusion of communities, Sun Ra made seemingly disparate aesthetics—the diurnal activities of the store and the sci-fi dress code and spacey sounds of the music—complementary.

The way Sun Ra operated has influenced how Ayewa inhabits the persona of Moor Mother while running the AfroFuturist Affair. Lyrics to the opening track of *Jazz Codes*, "Umzansi," refer to the city within the context of Afrofuturism: "Aerospace agency, North-Philly satellite." Since "collaboration to me is community," insists Ayewa, her collaboration with other musicians and producers has been a fundamental part of the way community is embedded in a track.[14] "I wrote a new poetry book called *Jazz Codes*, and I reached out to a producer friend of mine that had some really beautiful dusty jazz loops."[15] While the Swedish producer Olof Melander goes on to produce the entire *Jazz Codes* LP, leading with the lyrics in this way can create difficulties. "The hard part is, 'Can I sing this right? Can I get a decent recording of me performing this correctly?'"[16] Eventually, Ayewa assembles ten tracks from the poems and wrestles with them, realizing more collaborators are needed to transform them into complete tracks. "Then I started to reach out to some of my friends in Philly and have 'em come over and sing something."[17]

One friend in the community Ayewa chooses to collaborate with is Wolf Weston. Revealing the breadth of her dynamic vocal range, Weston's group, Saint Mela, release their EP *I Have No Fantasies to Sell You* the same year as *Jazz Codes*. Once the vocalists and musicians lay down their parts, Ayewa and Melander manipulate them and turn the songs into complete tracks. "The live playing doesn't always go to what the people think they're playing to. Things get moved around. Sometimes maybe the flute works with this [other thing] better, you know?"[18] Individual contributions are like pieces of a jigsaw puzzle with no predetermined design: "It's more like orchestrating once you get all the pieces."[19]

With *Jazz Codes* and its immediate predecessor, 2020's *Black Encyclopedia of the Air*, Ayewa drops the abrasiveness of earlier Moor Mother LPs—though 2024's *The Great Bailout* pursues it—in favor of exploring a softer dynamic range, adding a further genre by fusing jazz and hip-hop with neo-soul. "I'm constantly going into different genres and fields to make the message more accessible," says Ayewa.[20] "This was just the mood of these two records.

They're really soft. And I was nervous about that because I like noise."[21] Softness could bring Ayewa close to a more stylistic, slick, type of fusion of jazz and hip-hop and soul, but Moor Mother's LPs avoid this by using softness strategically. "This record is like a gateway, a trickery," says Ayewa, "I like to punch people in the heart and then kiss the heart."[22] The self-confessed trickery ensures the tension essential to fusion is maintained. In this sense, the emphasis on process in the composing, recording, and editing of the tracks is transferred to the listener, as they are drawn into the music and then startled. Operating as a reverberating time machine collecting dust as it travels, "Evening" remains distinctive in Moor Mother's discography.

1. Camae Ayewa, quoted in Madison Bloom, "Moor Mother on How Her New Album is a Gateway to Radical Thought," *Pitchfork* (September 2, 2021), https://pitchfork.com/thepitch/moor-mother-black-encyclopedia-of-the-air-interview/.
2. For Ayewa's comments on Butler, see Moor Mother (lecture, Red Bull Music Academy, Berlin, 2018), https://www.redbullmusicacademy.com/lectures/moor-mother-lecture.
3. Mark Dery, "Black to the Future," in *Flame Wars: The Discourse of Cyberculture* (Durham, NC: Duke University Press, 1994), 180.
4. Gabriel Solis, "Soul, Afrofuturism and the Timeliness of Contemporary Jazz Fusions," *Daedalus* 148, no. 2 (Spring 2019): 23–35.
5. Olivia Giovetti, "Closing the Timeline: An Interview with Moor Mother," *VAN Magazine* (September 1, 2022), https://van-magazine.com/mag/moor-mother/.
6. Nina Simone, quoted in *What Happened, Miss Simone?*, directed by Liz Garbus (Los Angeles: Netflix, 2015).
7. Moor Mother (lecture, Red Bull Music Academy).
8. Ibid.
9. See Nate Patrin, *Bring That Beat Back: How Sampling Built Hip-Hop* (Minneapolis, MN: Minnesota University Press, 2020).
10. Camae Ayewa, quoted in Phil Freeman, "Ugly Beauty: The Month in Jazz," *Stereogum* (July 19, 2020), https://www.stereogum.com/2193524/moor-mother-jazz-codes-interview/columns/ugly-beauty/.

11. Camae Ayewa, quoted in Jordan Darville, "Moor Mother on Collaboration, Community, and the Power of Sampling," *Fader*, https://www.thefader.com/2021/09/21/moor-mother-on-collaboration-community-and-the-power-of-sampling.
12. Moor Mother (lecture, Red Bull Music Academy).
13. Ibid.
14. Ayewa, quoted in Darville, "Moor Mother on Collaboration, Community."
15. Ayewa, quoted in Bloom, "Gateway to Radical Thought."
16. Moor Mother (lecture, Red Bull Music Academy).
17. Ayewa, quoted in Freeman, "Ugly Beauty."
18. Ibid.
19. Ibid.
20. Ayewa, quoted in Bloom, "Gateway to Radical Thought."
21. Ibid.
22. Ibid.

The Comet Is Coming, "Pyramids" (2022)

Sensibilities

"Pyramids" fuses spiritual jazz with electronica
by bringing together the sensibilities of the Comet
Is Coming's three members: Dan Leavers on
synthesizer and keyboards, Shabaka Hutchings
on tenor saxophone, and Max Hallett on drums.
So thorough is the fusion of each band member's
approach to playing that it's impossible to
differentiate them. They frequently swap roles

by adopting each other's instruments via their own: when Leavers's synthesizer assumes the role of lead, Hutchings provides rhythmic texture as a synth often does; and when Hallett solos on tom-toms, Leavers provides a constant pulse in the background as a kick drum would. The sonic heart to "Pyramids" is the way each musician extracts the maximum "resonance," as Hutchings called it, from their instrument while also affording the other members the freedom to do the same.[1]

"Pyramids" opens slowly with Leavers's synthesizer leading. Forty seconds in, Hutchings enters on saxophone, sounding a sequence of sharp, repetitive honks. Next, Leavers introduces a second layer of synthesizer, and the track feels on the verge of exploding as Hallett's drumming intensifies, but the music loops back to the quieter passage the track began with instead. After the sequence is repeated, the energy starts to build a second time only to dissipate again. The third time around, an identical pattern emerges until, finally, Leavers unleashes a miasmic monster of a riff, which Hutchings replies to in kind and Hallett accompanies with a euphoric drum fill.

The Comet Is Coming formed in 2013 when Hutchings spontaneously joined Leavers and Hallett onstage while they were performing as electronic duo Soccer96. "[We] began to notice a tall [...] figure present at some of our gigs and at some point he appeared at the side of the stage with his sax in hand."[2] Beckoned onstage, Hutchings improvised over the music, creating what Hallett emphatically refers to as "an explosive shockwave of energy."[3] An instant connection was formed between the three musicians. "It was one of those stars aligning kind of moments," enthuses Leavers, "where you're like 'yeah, we've all got a similar intensity.'"[4] They began rehearsing together at the Total Refreshment Centre in northeast London, soon settling on the name the Comet Is Coming, purloined from a 1960s BBC Radiophonic Workshop track. "Once we heard this piece, with its allusions to sci-fi, cosmic remembrances, and general space," recalls Hutchings, "it instantly struck a chord."[5] Pseudonyms appearing to derive from the same source were soon adopted by each band member: Betamax for Hallett, Danalogue for Leavers, and King Shabaka for Hutchings. The trio released an EP in 2015 and their first LP a year later, followed by a second in 2019, and *Hyper-Dimensional Expansion Beam*—the LP with "Pyramids"—in 2022.

Hutchings's notion of "resonance" emerges from listening to the spiritual jazz of Pharoah Sanders, a tenor saxophonist known for his impassioned playing that combined overblowing with multiphonics. "Although I've been listening to Pharoah for a long time, it's only in the last five years that I've become really sensitized and able to feel the full resonance he extracts from the saxophone."[6] After John Coltrane's *Love Supreme* (1965), and live work featuring Alice Coltrane on keyboards and Sanders on tenor saxophone, spiritual jazz gained pace in the late 1960s. Born in London but raised primarily in Barbados, Hutchings was attracted to spiritual jazz and Sanders in his teens, particularly appreciating the way the saxophonist worked in unison with other musicians. "The resonance of Pharoah's tenor doesn't come at the cost of the other musicians drawing the maximum resonance from theirs," remarks Hutchings.[7] "Mantra," from Alice Coltrane's *Ptah, the El Daoud* (1970), highlights the way Sanders alternates between intense passages that draw attention to the saxophone and quieter ones, giving space to Coltrane's keyboard and Ron Carter's bass. From Sanders, Hutchings also heeds the lesson of when to not play; there are moments in "Pyramids" when the saxophone is silent, allowing the synthesizer and drums to resonate.

Running parallel with spiritual jazz in the early 1970s is the development of electronic music. Leavers describes how "everything from Kraftwerk to Detroit techno" feeds into his keyboard and synthesizer playing.[8] Leavers approaches electronic music by drawing on the way 1980s Detroit techno producers Carl Craig and Juan Atkins channel Kraftwerk ("they were so stiff, they were funky," Craig remarked).[9] Each of these producers sped up and deepened the Düsseldorf-based band's repetitive beats to the point where they became hypnotic—that is, ripe for dancing to. Seeing how audiences respond to "Pyramids" live in 2023 gives a sense of the importance of dancing to the Comet Is Coming.

Hallett retools aspects of drumming from electronic music and spiritual jazz, accommodating both Hutchings's saxophone and Leavers's synthesizer. Influenced by a drummer known for fusion, Jack DeJohnette, Hallett is particularly attracted to how he moves between electric-era Miles Davis with cuts such as the funky "Spanish Key" from 1970's *Bitches Brew* and the spiritual jazz of Alice Coltrane on 1974's *Illuminations*. DeJohnette extracted the maximum resonance from his drum kit while allowing the other musicians to do the same on their instruments.

Though not mentioned by any of the band's members, saxophonist Joe Farrell's overlooked track

"Night Dancing" from 1978 operates like a futuristic trailer for the Comet Is Coming's "Pyramids." Featuring both the synthesizer and the saxophone, the track fuses the histories of electronic music and spiritual jazz that feed into "Pyramids" while emphasizing the distinctiveness of each instrument. Released a year after Kraftwerk's *Trans-Europe Express* (and Giorgio Moroder and Donna Summer's "I Feel Love"), Jeff Porcaro's metronomic beat on "Night Dancing" accompanies Michael Porcaro's synthesizer and Farrell's tenor saxophone in a way that is distinctive for the time. Herbie Hancock or George Duke may have already set synthesizers to repetitive drumbeats with a saxophone playing over the top ("Quasar" from 1972's *Crossings* or "Dawn" from 1975's *The Aura Will Prevail* both come to mind), but "Night Dancing" is one of the first tracks to sync a saxophone and a synthesizer in this way.

Like the process of these musicians from the 1970s, the Comet Is Coming's writing and recording is essential to how they extract the maximum possible from their respective instruments. "We write collaboratively as a group and we trust each other to work out parts that complement each other," explains Hallett.[10] "The main objective is to create a highly creative situation where ideas are able to flow freely and spontaneously, and capture those moments."[11] To remove preconceived patterns of playing and composing, the band arrives at the recording studio with no music previously written. Everything happens in the studio with all three members present. In the daytime they "start to work out little bits and ideas and basically record as we go," then "as we get into the evening we start recording free jams."[12] Structuring their studio time by oscillating between playing specific passages and open-ended jams leads the band to tracks such as "Pyramids."

After a few days of playing, the band amass hours of recordings. "Sometimes for a track that ends up being four minutes long, we may have played it, or played an improvisation that included those moments, for half an hour."[13] Time spent reviewing the recordings is as important as playing. "Maybe we're listening back in the studio, everyone's really kind of feeling a section, really vibing out [so] we'll […] earmark that."[14] Sometimes, it's only during "the process of mixing and producing that certain tracks reveal themselves to be a true statement that didn't seem like it before."[15] With the recording studio having been a vital creative tool for the band, it is essential they edit and produce the tracks themselves.

What's distinctive about *Hyper-Dimensional Expansion Beam* is its attempt to channel the energy of the band's concerts into a recording. "We tend to have these really intense gigs," enthuses Leavers, "so with this record, we wanted to unite the live sound and the studio sound a little bit more."[16] The band found that the best way to do this is not to record a precomposed track live in the studio or capture a live concert but to carefully edit the hours of recordings amassed and shape them. The way each musician extracts the maximum resonance from their instrument is vital to the intensity the band is looking for. Artist Daniel Martin Diaz's cover for *Hyper-Dimensional Expansion Beam* captures this by incorporating the spiritual and the technological elements of the band within a diagrammatic cosmic map.

Reflecting their broad listening habits, each band member speaks highly reflexively about the notion of genre. Where Leavers describes the band's music as "kind of devoid from genre," Hallett insists on there being "no genre boundaries."[17] Hutchings is more expansive, especially in relation to the era of music he draws from. "There was a lot of self-consciousness about fusion coming from the society around the musicians of the 1960s and 1970s rather than the musicians themselves. Even though we may not have stepped over those boundaries, we're no longer talking about them as if they are real."[18] While extracting elements from diverse genres across these periods, the fusion between spiritual jazz and electronic music taking place on "Pyramids" feels totally intuitive as each musician moves fluidly.

With fusion being an ongoing process of change, it's no coincidence that, after being together for a decade, the Comet Is Coming play their final concerts in autumn of 2023. With the turn into 2024, Leavers presses forward on a forthcoming synth-driven solo LP, Hutchings puts aside the saxophone and takes up the flute on his solo LP *Perceive Its Beauty, Acknowledge Its Grace*, and Hallett focuses on his band Champagne Dub. With fusion as process, change is endemic.

1. Shabaka Hutchings, interview with the author, May 2023.
2. Max Hallett, interview with the author, January 2024.
3. Ibid.
4. Dan Leavers, quoted in "How the Comet Is Coming Channel the Collaborative Spirit of Jazz," *Crack Magazine* (June 21, 2019), https://www.youtube.com/watch?v=IkE8sCaP4h8.
5. Hutchings, quoted in "Into the Mystic," Marlbank (October 23, 2013), https://archive.marlbank.net/gigs/1176-the-comet-is-coming-xoyo-london-17-november.
6. Hutchings, interview with the author.
7. Ibid. In September 2023, Hutchings performed Sanders's role in *Promises* (2022) with Floating Points in a concert at the Hollywood Bowl, shortly after Sanders's death.
8. Dan Leavers, interview with the author, March 2023.

9. Carl Craig, quoted in Simon Reynolds, "A Tale of Three Cities," in *Energy Flash: A Journey Through Rave Music and Dance Culture* (Picador: London, 1998), 3.

10. Max Hallett, quoted in Klemen Breznikar, "The Comet Is Coming Interview," *It's Psychedelic Baby Magazine* (February 25, 2020), https://www.psychedelicbabymag.com/2020/02/the-comet-is-coming-interview.html.

11. Ibid.

12. Ibid.

13. Dan Leavers, quoted in Max Pilley, "The Comet Is Coming: 'The Scene Is A Construct,'" *Loud and Quiet* (September 26, 2022), https://www.loudandquiet.com/interview/the-comet-is-coming-the-scene-is-a-construct/.

14. Dan Leavers, quoted in "Collaborative Spirit of Jazz."

15. Ibid.

16. Leavers, quoted in Pilley, "The Comet Is Coming."

17. Leavers, quoted in ibid.; Hallett, interview with the author.

18. Hutchings, interview with the author.

Outro

Tracks under consideration for *Fusion!!*
From George Duke to Moses Boyd

Betty Carter, "Two Cigarettes in the Dark" (1963)
Duke Ellington, "Afro-Bossa" (1963)
Quincy Jones, "Walking in Space" (1969)
George Duke, "For Love (I Come Your Friend)" (1975)
Ryo Kawasaki, "Joni" (1975)
Lalo Schifrin, "Black Widow" (1976)
The Style Council, "Dropping Bombs on the
Whitehouse" (1984)
Goldie, "Still Life" (1995)
Erykah Badu, "Amerykahn Promise" (2008)
Moses Boyd, "Stranger Than Fiction" (2020)
DOMi and JD Beck, "Whatup" (2022)
Amirtha Kidambi's Elder Ones, "The Great Lie" (2024)

Acknowledgments

Early versions of chapters have appeared as articles in *DAMN°* and *We Jazz*, and as lectures for Whitechapel Gallery, London, the 92nd St Y, New York, and the Music for Girls conference, University of Sussex.

Thanks to everyone at Sternberg Press, especially Caroline Schneider for commissioning the book; Emma Capps, Lucy Brown, and Marta Gaspar; and my incredible and patient editor Leah Whitman-Salkin.

To Fraser Muggeridge and Manon Veyssière for the design.

To Neil Arthur, Tom Berry, David Blamey, Moses Boyd, James Dyer, Jonathan Faiers, Richard Farrow, Gary Finnegan, Mike Heneghan, HH, Dale Holmes, Charlie Jackson, Gabrielle Kennedy, KL, Dan Leavers, Derrick Lloyd McLean, Magda Maculewicz, Simon Oliver, Rick Poyner, Sean Roe, Barry Schwabsky, Nick Simonin, Steve Swindells, and Tom Wilcox for help along the way.

To Kevin Fellezs at Columbia University, Steven F. Pond at Cornell University, Pierre Alexandre Tremblay at the University of Huddersfield, Tony Whyton at Birmingham City University, and Justin A. Williams at the University of Bristol for their insights into the histories of jazz.

Special thanks to Sophie McKinlay and Rupert Howe for reading the entire manuscript countless times.

Colophon

Alex Coles
Fusion!
From Alice Coltrane to Moor Mother

Published by Sternberg Press

Editor: Leah Whitman-Salkin
Proofreaders: Blanche Craig and Anita Iannacchione
Design: Fraser Muggeridge and Manon Veyssière
Main typeface: Library by Pierre Pané-Farré
Additional typefaces: Portrait and Plantin
Inside cover: Fraser Muggeridge, *Iceland Squeegee*, 2024
Printer: Tallinn Book Printers, Estonia

ISBN 978-1-915609-37-3

Distributed by The MIT Press, Art Data, Les presses
du réel, and Idea Books.

Sternberg Press
71–75 Sheldon Street
London WC2H 9JQ
www.sternberg-press.com

Sternberg Press

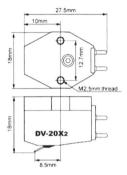

All vinyl played using a Dynavector cartridge.